RMS TITANIC

The First Violin

The life, loves and loss
of the great liner's bandsman
John Law Hume
by his great niece
Yvonne Hume
with a foreword by Millvina Dean, Titanic's last survivor

First Published in the United Kingdom, 2011
Stenlake Publishing Limited
54-58 Mill Square, Catrine, KA5 6RD
01290 551122
www.stenlake.co.uk

ISBN 978 1 84033 551 4

This is a revised edition of the hardback edition of the book *RMS Titanic 'The First Violin'* ISBN 978 1 84033 521 7.

By the same author.

RMS Titanic 'Dinner is Served'
ISBN 978 1 84033 484 5

visit her website.
www.yvonnehume.co.uk

Stenlake Publishing Ltd.

CONTENTS

Foreword	4
Introduction	5
Queen of the South	6
Musical Heritage	10
The Liners	20
The Musicians	32
Leaving Dumfries (part)	44-48
colour section	49-64
Leaving Dumfries (continued)	65
The Iceberg	68
The Aftermath	78
Epilogue	88
Millvina Dean	90
Selection of White Star Music	93
Acknowledgements	96

Foreword

"I felt very honoured when I was asked to write a foreword to a book about the extremely brave men in the orchestra of the ill-fated Titanic.

They are an inspiration to everyone and I'm sure they will never be forgotten"

Millvina Dean
2nd February 1912 – 31st May 2009

Youngest Titanic Survivor

Introduction

I have lovingly and with great pride written this book as a tribute to my great uncle, John Law Hume, the first violinist with the band on board the *Titanic*. The bravery of one so young and his selfless actions of continuing to play, along with the other members of the band when the *Titanic* was sinking, enabled some passengers to meet their impending death with serenity and acceptance, rather than panic.

The Hume story is a fascinating one and although it has been a very emotional journey for me, I have thoroughly enjoyed looking deeper into my family history, which has revealed many interesting surprises. The story goes to 1914 and has not stopped at 1912, as intertwined within John's fascinating life is a moving and gripping love story.

Yvonne Hume

Queen of the South

Dumfries is the largest town in the south west of Scotland and has a population of approximately 35,000. The town is the administrative centre of Dumfries and Galloway and sits on the east side of the River Nith, with Maxwelltown to the west. Its early history was very turbulent, with Picts, Saxons and Danes all fighting for control of the area during the 7th to 9th centuries. In 1186, during the reign of William 1st of Scotland, Dumfries was granted the status of Royal Burgh. The land on the other side of the Nith (Galloway) continued to be part of England until 1234, thus making Dumfries important as a border town. During its first fifty years it grew to become an important market town and port. On 10th February 1306 Robert the Bruce killed a rival for the Scottish Crown, John III Comyn

Dumfries from Maxwelltown.

(The Red Comym) in the church of the Grey Friars, and although he was excommunicated he still went on to become king. The present Greyfriars church at the west end of High Street was built in 1868 and overlooks Burns' statue.

Devorgilla Bridge, the first bridge over the Nith was built in 1432 and was named after Lady Devorgilla who was King John Balliol's mother. Over the centuries it has been rebuilt more than once; it is one of the oldest bridges in Scotland and today it is used by pedestrians only. The New Bridge, linking Buccleuch Street and Galloway Street was designed by architect Thomas Boyd and completed in 1793. One hundred years later, it was widened by engineer Sir William Arrol, from a design by the noted architect Thomas Barbour.

Cattle market on the Whitesands.

Dumfries has, through the centuries, thrived as a busy market town. A charter was signed by Robert III in 1395, giving the townspeople the rights and responsibilities in running a market. A further charter, signed by James VI in 1621, gave the town the right to hold a market on two days of the week. These markets were held in Queensberry Square and the High Street, but these moved to Whitesands, the site of the former cattle market in the twentieth century. The town has had its fair share of notoriety over the centuries, including in 1659 when nine women were burned to death for practising witchcraft. The striking Mid Steeple in the High Street was built in 1707 as a courthouse and prison. As a reminder of the town's history as a wool and cloth trading centre on the front of the building is carved an 'ELL' (37 inches), which is an old Scottish measurement for wool and cloth.

The most famous person to live in Dumfries was Scotland's National Poet Robert Burns. He moved to the town in 1791 after he gave up the tenancy of Ellisland Farm, a few miles outside of Dumfries to the north. For a time he was employed as Customs Officer to the port, which despite being several miles inland from the sea, had established trade with colonies in North America. He moved into a house in Mill Street, after living for a while in three rooms of a house in what is now Bank Street. During his time in the town Burns was a regular visitor to the Theatre Royal in Shakspeare Street, which he helped raise subscriptions to build. He also frequented the Globe Inn in the High Street. Not long before his death in 1796 he wrote of the Globe *the Globe Tavern here, which these many years has been my Howff...*

The house in which he was living when he died in is now a museum and the street has been renamed Burns Street. Jean, his wife, continued to live in the house until her death in 1834.

The port of Dumfries started to decline in the mid-nineteenth century with the advent of the railways. The increasing size of trading ships, coupled with the river's unpredictable tides, made navigation almost impossible. In 1832 Dumfries, in common with the rest of Great Britain and much of the world, suffered from an outbreak of Asiatic cholera. The disease first struck on 15th September. Mrs. Mary Paterson contracted the disease and died the following day. The town was declared clear on 27th November. At least 900 people died, including 44 recorded deaths in one day. Of all those that were infected, less than 415 recovered. There is a monument to this epidemic in the churchyard of St. Michael's Church.

The dock of the port of Dumfries.

The town gained its affectionate nickname of "Queen Of The South" in 1857 when local poet David Dunbar, who was standing for Parliament in the election of that year, was giving an address and referred to the town as his 'Queen Of The South'. The name stuck and in 1919 when several local football clubs merged to form one the most popular name was 'Queen Of The South', still the name of the local professional football team. In 1875 a suspension footbridge that crosses the Nith just west of the entrance to Dock Park was opened.

Although not a major manufacturing centre, Dumfries nevertheless had a number of industries in the 19th century. On the southern side of the Nith there were two tweed mills, Troqueer and Rosefield. On the opposite side of the river beyond Dock Park were the Nithsdale (woollen) Mills. Other industries sprang up as a by-product of the wool trade, including hat-making and a booming hosiery business, with two factories across the river in Maxwelltown. Smaller industry included shoe and clog making, brewing, tanning and basket-making. There was also a large foundry which made steam engines, boilers, plant for railways and iron for the construction of bridges. In 1913 the Arrol Johnston car company opened a factory in Heathall, on the outskirts of the town. It was reputedly very similar to

Troqueer Mill. The suspension bridge can just be made out in the background.

the Ford factory in Michigan where the Model T was built. Car production was halted in 1914 when production of aero engines commenced with the outbreak of war. The factory is still in use today manufacturing carpet underlay. Until recently it had manufactured the famous 'Hunters' green wellington boots.

In the late 19th century Whitesands, on the banks of the Nith, was home every March to the Rood Fair. Originally this consisted of stalls but was later replaced by sideshows and fairground rides and it would seem the whole town would converge on this part of the town. The fair was on the site of the cattle market. Nowadays the fair is still going but is very small by comparison.

Crowds and sideshows at the Rood Fair.

Musical Heritage

The musical beginnings of John Law Hume were due to his inherited family talent. His grandather, also named John, was a general labourer who had a certain level of musical ability on the violin. John Hume Senior was working on a farm in the tiny village of Haugh of Urr, south west of Dumfries and not far from the town of Castle Douglas, when he married Ellen Halliday on 8th December 1854. Soon afterwards they moved to the village of Closeburn (about ten miles north of Dumfries) where John got work on another farm and their first child Ebenezer was born on 17th July 1856. He was followed by James (1858), Mary (1859), and Ellen (1861). By the time Andrew was born on 7th May 1864 the family had

Haugh of Urr.

moved to the small village of Lochfoot, four miles to the west of Dumfries. Another child, Maggie, was born in 1868 before the Humes moved to the the tiny hamlet of Cherrytrees, a mile or so to the east of Dumfries. This hamlet consisted of a row of just four cottages and was located opposite the asylum, the Crichton Royal Institute. In 1871 John started work as an attendant at the Crichton, eventually becoming a night inspector. Two more children, Jessie and Lily, were born in 1871 and 1873 respectively.

Lochfoot village.

As a child Andrew began to show promise as a talented musician, especially on the violin which he alse became very adept at repairing. After his schooling and while still in his teens he moved to London to study under Prosper Philippe Sainton, a prominent violinist and composer of the time. While studying there Andrew began to make violins as a hobby. He decided to develop his skills in violin manufacture and spent the summer months at violin centres in Saxony and in Bohemia (today part of the Czech Republic). Once he was trained, Andrew moved to Glasgow to pursue a career in classical music and violin making. He was living in the Kelvinside district of the city when he met and fell in love with laundress Grace Law, the 21year old daughter of the family living next door. At the age of 23 he had become a tall, handsome man with a full moustache and perhaps exciting tales of life in London and beyond. On 23rd July 1887 Andrew and Grace were married in a simple Church of Scotland ceremony at 53, Mount Street, Glasgow. Not long after starting their married life the newlyweds decided to move some 60 miles south to the smaller market town of Dumfries. It was at 38 Academy Street, on the southern side of a bend in the River Nith, opposite the author J.M. Barrie's former school, Dumfries Academy, that Andrew and Grace made their home, typical of many at the time, being a terraced house that was split into upstairs and ground level flats – basic accommodation but quite adequate for the young couple.

Over the coming months Andrew built a reputation for being a very adept musician and composer, proving to be a popular and capable teacher, providing lessons from the cosy

Academy Street, Dumfries.

front room of the house. On occasions he would be called upon to make a violin and he would toil away for hours on end at the kitchen table. It was during these months that Grace was preparing for motherhood and on 30th April 1888, some nine months after their wedding, that the couple's first child was born, a healthy baby daughter whom they named Nellie.

In the summer of the following year the family moved half a mile or so to the other side of town to 5 Nith Place, one street back from the river. This time home was a two storey house above a haircutters shop and although the area was less salubrious, the house was larger than the one in Academy Street. Andrew continued to make a living from his music, frequently spending a night away from home to play at different venues in the west of Scotland, while Grace was managing the home and raising young Nellie. On Sundays the family worshipped at the Waterloo Place Congregational Church, an imposing red sandstone building looking out across the river, which was just a short walk from their home on the corner of Nith Place and Whitesands. The building is still there today and is currenly used by the Salvation Army.

Both Andrew and Grace were active members of the church; Andrew played the violin, bassoon or banjo, in the "Band of Hope", regularly walking the streets playing their music. Over the years the couple became close friends with the Reverend James Strachan who had been minister at the church since 1870.

In the winter of 1889 Grace found out she was expecting her second child. At 6.45am on 9th August 1890, on what was to be a beautiful summer's day, Grace and Andrew's first son and my great uncle, was born. Andrew was delighted that he now had a son and it was decided to call the baby John, after Andrew's father, with the middle name Law, from Grace's maiden name.

Two years later, as Nellie was enjoying her childhood and preparing to begin her education at the local school in Glebe Street, John was a typical two year old who had a head of blond curly hair and a cheeky smile! The musical blood had been passed to Nellie too, as she took an interest in music by learning the piano. On 26th August 1892 the family grew further still with the arrival of another daughter, Grace. With five mouths to feed now Andrew took on extra work making and repairing furniture. The daily toil was long as he had to juggle his teaching, composing, instrument making and playing in the church band. Life in the late 19th century was certainly hard.

As his birthday fell in August, John was a year later than most starting school. This extra time spent at home was where he began to develop his passion for music, the banjo being first followed by the violin. In August 1895 the five year old John Hume enrolled at the small St. Michael Street School in Glebe Street, Dumfries. St. Michael's Primary School as it is today is still educating youngsters from the area. It was only a five minute walk from the family home in Nith Place, along the Kirkgate past St. Michael's Church, the final resting place of the poet Robert Burns.

John aged 7, centre row, third from the left.

Starting school at the same time as John was another boy by the name of Tom (Thomas) Mullin, who went on to become a steward in the Third Class section of the *Titanic*. Although they were not in the same class at school they did play in the same football team. The headmaster, John Hendrie, got to know young John very well and once remarked that he was "a bright, laughing, pleasant boy who always had a merry outlook on life". A marble memorial plaque situated in the hallway of St. Michael's Primary School is a permanent reminder of the two former pupils and their heroic deeds.

John became one of the most popular pupils at school, always happy and smiling whilst seizing every chance to play the violin, his friends looking on with pride as their chubby cheeked friend with his trademark curls raised his violin to his chin. John loved to perform and his friends loved watching him play. He had school during the week, Sunday school at the weekend and violin practice in the evenings. At Sunday school in the Waterloo Place Congregational Church John gave his first public performance on the violin, under the watchful and no doubt proud eyes of his parents!

The cottages of Springbank from across the Nith.

It was soon time to move home again and in 1896 the family moved to 4 Springbank, Dumfries. This was a pretty white painted house in a row of four, with the gardens of the rather grand Nith House on one side and the carriage works building on the other. The house overlooked the river and the busy market place where farmers from the surrounding area would come to buy and sell livestock. It was a larger house (as it needed to be to accommodate the growing family) and was also closer to their place of worship. During the time the Humes were living here the properties along Whitesands were all renumbered and 4 Springbank became 84 Whitesands. The family grew further when on 28th June 1897 Grace gave birth to another daughter called Catherine, named after Grace's mother. The household was very busy now with Nellie, John and Grace receiving their schooling and practising music in the evenings and Andrew teaching music from home. Unfortunately on 11th December 1898 John's 66 year old grandfather, John, died from stomach cancer. In the spring of 1901 the family moved back to Nith Place, this time to number nine, which was a two storey house above Mr. Milligan's flesher (butcher) shop.

With Andrew being a passionate musician and active member of the community he was always looking for ways to play in public and raise funds for local causes. One of these opportunities arose on June 19th 1901, when the *Dumfries and Galloway Standard*, a local newspaper still going strong, carried the following letter:

Sir,- As the summer months are now here. I would like to make a suggestion as regards to music in the park- that a string band be formed to discourse music on the stand, say, Tuesday nights. This would be a novelty and a variation from the brass band. I think it would be very much appreciated by the public. I may say that I have spoken to a few musicians who would give their services gratis. The first part of the program could be devoted to selections, and the latter half entirely to dance music. What do our musical enthusiasts think of the above suggestion?- Yours, &c. MUSICIAN

Three days later on the 22nd a reply that Andrew had written appeared in the newspaper, under the heading MUSIC IN THE PARK:

Sir,- Re "Musician's" suggestion on above subject in your issue of the 19th inst., an orchestra would no doubt be a novelty and a variation to the brass band. There might be difficulty in getting a sufficiently strong number of capable strings together to enable a good program to be presented. Personally, I should not mind giving, say, an experimental night, provided an unreasonable amount of time would not be required for rehearsals. If players will send in their names they can have their parts immediately .-Yours, &c., A. HUME. 9 Nith Place.

The park in question is Dock Park, situated between St. Michael's Street and the River Nith. Just a few yards from the bandstand now stands a granite obelisk that is a memorial to John Hume and Thomas Mullin. This was the setting for young John to enjoy his first taste of playing in a string ensemble, at the tender age of nine. Reverend Strachan, minister of his local church, commented when he saw him play; "a cooler young fellow he never knew when about to play". The foundations were now laid for a career as a professional musician and the travel experiences that followed. Throughout the summer months Andrew organised several concerts from the bandstand for strings, with young John being included and no doubt loving every moment!

The bandstand in Dock Park.

During these months that Grace was pregnant for the fifth and final time and on 4th November 1901, my grandfather Andrew was born. The rich vein of musical talent that ran through the family continued with my grandfather and he went on to become a professional musician, regularly touring the country in the years between the wars. He was always billed as 'Andy Hume and his boys'.

Around this time, John started performing on his own in front of audiences in the intimate surroundings of the Shakespeare Street Theatre, prior to the curtain rising on the main performance and again during the interval. To most this would have been a daunting experience, but John had such confidence in his own ability that he just took it all in his stride, prompting some of his friends to say when they saw him play here that they fully expected him to "fiddle his way to fame".

Top left: Theatre Royal in Shakespeare Street.

Above: Interior of the Theatre Royal.

Left: Andrew Hume, John's father.

Over the next two years or so, the fortunes of the family went in two directions. Andrew was established as a professor of music on the violin, bassoon and banjo. His work took him away from the family frequently. Grace, however, suffered ill-health to such an extent that eventually she became virtually housebound. This was particularly difficult for all concerned, especially Nellie as being the eldest she would have been expected to help, not only around the home, but with her younger brother and sisters. John's grandmother, Ellen, would have helped where she could too, but as she was approaching her seventies, this would have been limited. Around this time the shop at number eleven, next to Milligan's butchers, was taken on by spinster Alice Alston and turned into a ladies and children's outfitter. She had moved from a more upmarket area of the town in Castle Street, lined with grand Georgian houses where she still lived with her parents. Her father had been in the woollen weaving business and her mother was a milliner. Over the months that followed Alice became a close friend of the Humes and wherever possible lent a helping hand.

English Street from the High Street.

In the summer of 1904 John left school, not long before he turned fourteen, and he began work as a clerk in the offices of solicitor James Geddes. The office was at 8 English Street, just off the southern end of the High Street, only a few minutes walk from his home in Nith Place. Although music was his life and he enjoyed nothing more than performing, he didn't envisage it being his future, much to the dismay of his father. John quickly settled into his daily routine and it wasn't long before he was receiving high praise from his boss. On several occasions his father tried to persuade him to leave the solicitor's office to concentrate on his music and it was on one of these occasions that Mr. Geddes told Andrew that his son was "intelligent, courteous and painstaking in all his work and was of a character that he could carve out a career in any walk of life that he chose to follow". Mr. Geddes probably realised that at some stage his loss would be music's gain!

John continued to work there for twelve months, but eventually found the confines of an office not to his liking and much to the delight of his father, John decided to devote his time to music. Andrew had always wanted John to be classically trained and to perform in orchestras, so at last it looked as if he would get his wish. By this time Grace's health was declining to such an extent that she was an invalid; Nellie, now out of school was expected to run the home and care for her mother, along with any help that Alice could give.

In the middle of April 1906 Grace became very ill and on 4th May she died at home from cancer of the throat, the last three weeks of her life being particularly traumatic for all concerned. Naturally all the family were devastated but none more so than Catherine, only eight years old and very close to her mother. A small obituary appeared in the *Dumfries and Galloway Standard*, stating that the funeral was to be held on May 7th at 1.15pm at St. Michael's Church, with the service conducted by Reverend Montgomery Campbell. Grace was buried in St. Michael's Cemetery, Rosevale Road in the same grave as Andrew's parents, John and Ellen Hume.

**St. Michael's Church from its old churchyard.
The cemetery in Rosevale Street is about half a mile away.**

Just after Christmas of 1906 Ellen, who by this time was 74 years old, contracted pneumonia and she died on 4th January 1907. Ellen was buried in the same grave as her husband John and daughter-in-law Grace. This was a very difficult time for the family, especially with Andrew still having to be away from home for work commitments. During this time the children became "very unruly", according to Andrew. Alice helped as much as possible, much to the annoyance of Catherine and to a lesser extent Nellie. Over the next year things got easier and Andrew and Alice decided to marry; they were both 43 years old, which was considered middle-aged at the time. On Friday 19th July 1907 the couple married, the ceremony taking place in St. Michael's Manse and presided over by Reverend Montgomery Campbell, who the previous year had officiated at Grace's funeral. Once they were married

Alice moved into the Humes' house next door at number nine. With Andrew teaching and Alice running her business, it was the first time the household had two incomes and it made a vast difference. However, nine year old Catherine was becoming very headstrong and disliked Alice whom she saw was trying to take the place of her mother and resented her imposition of discipline. It was also around this time that Nellie left home to live at 20 Devorgilla Terrace in Maxwelltown. Being the eldest, she had spent several years of her life looking after her siblings and caring for her mother, so to move out and be relieved of this would have been a welcome change. She started teaching music from home to make ends meet, but it wasn't long before she met 22 year old William Smith who owned the flesher (butcher) shop at 17 Market Square. Maxwelltown and on September 9th 1909, the two were married by Reverend James Strachan at Waterloo Place Manse, at a service in accordance with the forms of the Congregational Church. It was fitting that Reverend Strachan conducted the ceremony as by now he had known the family for more than twenty years.

St. Michael Street from Nith Place. The house at 5 Nith place is on the right of this view and the spire of St.Michael's Church dominates the background.

The Liners

In the early 1900s John would have seen advertising posters in Glasgow showing the glamorous new liners of the time and he may have heard stories from musicians that had played on them and decided that it was the life for him. His first posting at sea was on October 10th 1907 on board the Anchor Line's newest ship *California,* which sailed from Glasgow to New York via Moville (for Londonderry) in County Donegal, on the northern tip of Ireland. From the mid 19th century Moville was an important port of embarkation, especially for Irish emigrants travelling to New York and beyond, this call produced extra revenue for the Anchor Line. The head offices of the Anchor Line were at 12-16 St Vincent Place, Glasgow. This grand building was completed that same year, 1907, and today it is a listed building. With Glasgow being the Anchor Line's home port it was easy for John to return home between voyages.

The *California* was built in Glasgow by D&W Henderson Ltd., the same company that owned the Anchor Line. She was 470 feet long with a beam of 58 feet with a gross tonnage was 8,662. The ship was twin screw with the power coming from a six cylinder steam triple expansion engine which gave her a speed of sixteen knots. The captain for the maiden voyage was Captain J.Blakie.

The ship had an uneventful life until 28th June 1914 when it became stranded on Tory Island, off the coast of Donegal, where it stayed until August when it was taken to Glasgow to be repaired. In February 1917 she was torpedoed by a German U-Boat south of Fastnet Rock off southern Ireland and she sank with the loss of around forty lives.

As *California* was not a large vessel there would only have been four or five musicians onboard, comprising of two violins, viola and bass viol and if it were five, a cello. This would not have been daunting at all for John with his happy outgoing approach to life and confidence in his musical ability. He had played in public since an early age at his church, in Dock Park and the Theatre Royal and soon became a popular figure with all on board. Amongst the musicians there may well have been a bass viol player by the name of Louis Cross, who sailed with John on Cunard's *Carmania* on the last voyage he completed.

RMS *Celtic*, White Star Line.

John quickly got a taste of going to sea and built a reputation as being a musician of the highest calibre. During these transatlantic trips he started to make friends in New York. One can only speculate that he would have considered playing in orchestras there, once he had finished playing on the liners. By this time John was employed by the White Star Line that had sailed from Liverpool until it moved its main terminal to Southampton in 1907 (although some services remained at Liverpool). He would have moved because of all the talk amongst musicians he played alongside about the luxurious new 'super liners' of their day, the *Celtic*, *Cedric*, *Baltic* and *Adriatic*. These vast liners of their time, brought into service between 1901 and 1907 were known as The Big Four, with each being over 20,000 tons. They were capable of carrying huge numbers of passengers, notably in 3rd class, mainly emigrants to North America.

One of John's first trips for the White Star Line was on the smaller and ageing *Majestic,* which sailed from the new terminal at Southampton to New York via Cherbourg. This ship had her maiden voyage on April 2nd 1890, was 582 long with a beam of just under 58 feet and weighed 9,965 tons, and had twin propellers. On a westbound voyage to New York between 30th July and 5th August 1891, she won the coveted Blue Riband for the fastest crossing of the Atlantic, achieved with an average speed of 20.1 knots. She held this honour for only two weeks before her sister ship, *Teutonic,* completed the crossing with an average speed of 20.35 knots. In 1895 command of the ship was taken by an up and coming captain by the name of Edward Smith, who of course went on to be in command of the *Titanic*. In 1902 the *Majestic* underwent a refit including new boilers, which resulted in her having new taller funnels installed. She resumed service in 1903 and was eventually taken out of service in 1911 when the *Olympic* was completed, only to be again returned to service after the *Titanic* sank. She was sold for scrap in 1914.

SS *Majestic,* White Star Line, at Liverpool.

It wasn't long before John started to play on the larger and more luxurious ships in the White Star fleet. It was on the *Celtic*, the first of the Big Four, that John had his first taste of the large liners and when he possibly first met cellist John Carr, one of the many musicians who were hired by White Star. This ship was a regular on the Liverpool to New York run, sailing each time with five musicians who played as a quintet. John made many trips aboard White Star sailings from Liverpool, which was closer to home in Dumfries than Southampton, although on occasions he left from the south coast. This particular ship, *Celtic,* was launched on 4th April 1901 and was the first ship to be both longer and of a greater tonnage than the *Great Eastern*, built by Isambard Kingdom Brunel. Her length succeeded that of the *Oceanic*, which had held the title of the world's longest ship for two years. The maiden voyage of the *Celtic* was on 26th July 1901 on the Liverpool to New York run, although she also sailed from Southampton on a few occasions. The ship was a two funnel vessel driven by a quadruple expansion engine that produced 14,000 HP to twin propellers; she was not built for speed but for sheer luxury. In September of 1904 she carried 2,957 passengers on a westbound

RMS *Celtic*, leaving Liverpool.

Atlantic crossing, at that time the most that had been carried by White Star. During this period John and the all the musicians signed ship's articles, thus becoming members of the crew. When this was the case musicians tended to stay with one shipping line for longer. The wages at this time was £6.10s per month and although they provided their own uniform, an allowance of ten shillings a month was given. They were also allowed to keep a share of the gratuities. Between five musicians the tips were divided into six, with the bandmaster receiving two shares.

When back at home in Dumfries John continued to study his music at every opportunity and play alongside his father at venues around the area. Nellie meanwhile was working for J. L. Gibson & Co. a glove and hosiery manufacturer in Maxwell Street, Maxwelltown, to help supplement her music teaching. In April 1909 Alice, John's stepmother, sold her business to a Mrs. Jessie Elliott and along with Andrew, the family moved house again, this time to the more upmarket side of town at 42 George Street. This was a wide street, lined with impressive houses and just 150 yards from a bend in the river. They bought this house from the trustees of the late Mrs, Jane Murray and it was a marked improvement on anywhere that the Humes had lived before. A grand four storey double-fronted building constructed from the local red sandstone, it had six steps up to the large front door. The building sits on the corner of George Street and Castle Street, the street where Alice had lived before taking the shop in Nith Place. Today this building is the offices of Chartered Surveyors M. R. Rodgers and Partners and it still looks just as grand and imposing today as it would have done a century ago.

On one of John's trips home in early 1910 he met, according to Louis Cross, a "sweet young girl" by the name of Mary Costin, who lived at 35 Buccleuch Street, just two minutes walk from the Hume family home, directly opposite the courthouse and just a few doors up from

Buccleuch Street from the bridge, Dumfries.

the famous 'Barbours' outfitters and furnishers shop. Mary worked in the same glove and hosiery factory as John's sister Nellie. John and Mary would spend time walking in Greensands and it wasn't long before they fell in love and made plans to marry.

It had always been John's intention to give up going to sea, but maybe he curtailed it sooner than he had anticipated because of his love for Mary. In June 1910 he was one of five musicians on the *Megantic*, which sailed from Liverpool via Quebec to Montreal. The return trip left Montreal on 25th June and arrived in Liverpool on 1st July. The *Megantic* and her sister ship the *Laurentic* were built in the Belfast yards of Harland and Wolff . Originally they were ordered by Canada's Dominion Line and were to be called *Albany* and *Alberta*, but during construction they were transferred to the White Star Line. From 1902 these two lines were part of the International Mercantile Marine, a trust company that had been set up to monopolise international shipping trade, especially the transatlantic routes. IMM was the brainchild of the shipping magnates Clement Griscom (owner of the Red Star Line and American Line), Bernard N. Baker (owner of the Atlantic Transport Line), J. Bruce Ismay of the White Star Line and John Ellerman of the Leyland Line. The unprofitable Dominion Line was also amalgamated. This project was financed by J. P. Morgan. The two new ships, having been transferred to White Star, enabled IMM to start a service between Britain and Canada under the highly successful White Star flag. The formation of this trust caused panic within the British shipping industry and led directly to the British Government's subsidy of the Cunard Line's new ships *Lusitania* and *Mauretania* in order to compete.

Megantic was named after Lake Megantic in Quebec and was a single funnel ship, 550.4 feet long with a beam of 67.3 feet and tonnage of 14,878. She had the conventional two propellers, but the *Laurentic*, although sharing the same hull configuration, was fitted with three propellers of a new design. These two designs were an experiment for the upcoming Olympic class of ships that were on the drawing board. The *Megantic* was fitted out to a very high specification, in particular for wireless and submarine signalling devices, and also had refrigerating machinery and electric lighting. She undertook her maiden voyage on the Canadian route on 17th June 1909. In July 1910 John was on board on the return trip when one of the passengers was the notorious murderer, Dr. Hawley Harvey Crippen. He had been arrested while travelling to America on the *Montrose* just before it reached American soil. The captain of the *Montrose* had become suspicious of the behaviour of two passengers and before the ship was out of range of the wireless transmitter had radioed to London. The police officer in charge boarded the much faster *Laurentic* to make the arrests on 31st July. Crippen and his mistress Ethel le Neve were escorted back to England on the *Megantic*, which docked at Liverpool.

The idea for this new class of ship came about in 1907 when the chairman of Harland and Wolff invited Bruce Ismay and his wife Florence to dinner at his home in London. The idea was to compete with Cunard's *Mauretania* and *Lusitania*, not on speed but by setting new standards in luxury. The man in charge of overseeing the designing and building of the new Olympic Class of ship was Thomas Andrews, nephew of Lord Pirrie, a leading naval architect and managing director of Harland & Wolff. On 31st July an agreement was signed between Harland & Wolff and White Star to build three enormous triple screw ships. The third was to be called the *Gigantic*, but after the events of April 14th 1912 the name was changed to the *Britannic*. She wasn't launched until February 1914 and before she could commence transatlantic crossings the First World War broke out and she was requisitioned as a hospital ship. On 21st November 1916, just off the Greek island of Kea, she is thought to have hit a mine (but maybe was torpedoed) and sank. Working as a nurse on board at the time was Violet Jessop, who survived the sinking. She had been on the *Olympic* when it collided with the *Hawke* and on the *Titanic* when it sank.

***Olympic* under construction under the Great Gantry.**

The first two ships were to be built next to one another on a giant slipway called the Great Gantry. The hull numbers were to be 400 for the *Olympic* and 401 for the *Titanic*. The keel of the *Olympic* was laid in December 1908 and that of the *Titanic* was laid the following March.

This eased pressure on recruiting manpower and sourcing equipment for two such large ships. The *Olympic* was launched on 20th October 1910 and on 31st May 1911 the largest ship in the world, at 45,324 tons, was ready for duty. This was the same day that the *Titanic* was launched in Belfast. The *Olympic* departed on her maiden voyage on Wednesday 14th June 1911 with tens of thousands of onlookers gathered on the quayside. The fanfare surrounding the *Olympic* was far greater than that for the *Titanic* as she was the first of the new generation of liners. The five musicians would have assembled in the reception room to greet the First Class passengers as they boarded. The first port of call was Cherbourg followed by Queenstown, both to pick up mail and to board and disembark passengers, before setting sail for New York. She had five musicians. This was the first time John played on the same ship as cellist John Woodward, both employed because of their reputations of work on other ships, and a great honour for John who was only twenty years old at the time. The captain for the voyage was Edward Smith and joining him was First Officer William McMaster Murdoch who hailed from Dalbeattie, some twelve miles south west of Dumfries. He was highly regarded by White Star, having served on a number of their ships between 1900 and 1912. Murdoch was the centre of controversy when two films, in 1996 and 1997, portrayed him committing suicide after shooting two passengers dead who were trying to storm lifeboats. His home town was outraged, resulting in film studio executives visiting Dalbeattie, apologising to his relatives and donating £5,000 to a memorial fund set up in his honour. There is a granite plaque dedicated to him on the front of the town hall.

First Officer William Murdoch's memorial in Dalbeattie.

***Below*: The *Olympic*.**

With such a huge ship the musicians would have had very little free time during this maiden voyage as they had to play in different areas of the ship at different times of day, so the sight of the New York skyline on June 21st would have been a welcome one for John and the musicians. The ship was greeted by thousands of onlookers when she docked at Pier 59. Also onboard were Bruce Ismay and Thomas Andrews, with the latter accompanied by a group of Harland & Wolff engineers to check on any areas for improvement. The return trip was not until 28th June so it gave John plenty of time in New York to meet with friends and possibly attend concerts. The *Olympic* arrived back in Southampton on 5th July, with Ismay telling Lord Pirrie that the ship was a "marvel", with just one small aspect that could be improved on with the yet to be finished *Titanic*. First Class passengers had not been using the forward section of the promenade deck because they got wet when spray was thrown up from the bow. This was corrected before the *Titanic* sailed by enclosing the section with windows and adding extra cabins therefore making her the largest ship, just.

The Atlantic crossing of the *Olympic*, leaving Southampton on Wednesday 20th September was its fifth. John was once again employed, along with Woodward and another three musicians. Another person on board who was to become friendly with John was stewardess Violet Jessop who had also served on the *Majestic* at one time. Murdoch was again sailing as first officer and Hugh McElroy was again purser. At 11.25 am, with over 1,300 passengers onboard, the *Olympic* left her berth and headed towards the Isle of Wight. At 12.44 pm , the same time that HMS *Hawke* was just off Egypt Point, the northern tip of the Isle of Wight, her speed increased to sixteen knots Both ships were trying to travel down the same narrow stretch of water. The *Hawke* altered her course slightly to avoid a collision and she dropped back, but was then drawn into the *Olympic* by the suction of the huge propellers and crashed into her side. This resulted in two of Olympic's watertight compartments being flooded and damage to her propeller shaft. Meantime the bow of the *Hawke* was completely crushed. John Woodward and John had been playing draughts in their cabin, very close to the actual point of impact. Woodward later said that he had been so unconcerned about it that he continued with the game!

Damage caused to *Olympic* as a result of the HMS *Hawke* collision.

The ship limped back to Southampton for the damage to be assessed before she was taken to Belfast for repairs. The propeller shaft was replaced with one from the *Titanic* and work was halted on her to get the *Olympic* back into service as soon as possible. She was the pride of the White Star fleet and it was costing the company dearly to have her idle. During the course of these repairs John returned to Dumfries. When the ship finally returned to service on 20th November 1911 John was once again part of the quintet, despite Alice's fears. According to an interview Louis Cross later gave to the *New York Times* John had told the other musicians that after the *Olympic/Hawke* incident, Alice started to have dreams that he wasn't safe going to sea.

The following February the *Olympic* lost a propeller. Once again work was stopped on the nearly completed *Titanic* and one of her propellers used to repair her sister ship. This resulted in the maiden voyage of the *Titanic* being delayed from 20th March to 10th April.

The *Olympic* and *Titanic* (right) at Belfast, the *Titanic* is being moved out of the dry dock so that the *Olympic's* lost propellor can be replaced.

The *Olympic* was withdrawn from service in October 1912 for a refit to incorporate the lessons learned from the *Titanic* disaster. She was fitted with 64 wooden lifeboats along the boat deck, an inner watertight skin in the engine and boiler rooms, and the watertight bulkheads were extended up to B deck. She was also fitted with extra cabins on B deck. The result of these additions and alterations was to take her weight to 46,359 tons, 31 tons more than the *Titanic*. Probably the most unusual incident that occurred in her long career happened on 18th November 1929 when she was steaming very close to the last known position of the *Titanic* and began to shudder. This lasted for two minutes and was caused by a huge undersea earthquake on the Grand Banks two and a half miles beneath the surface. The earthquake was felt as far away as New York, and caused an undersea landslide that snapped twelve trans-Atlantic telegraph cables. The resulting tsunami killed 29 people and left 10,000 more homeless, in Newfoundland.

The *Olympic* became known as "Old Reliable" for her many years of service, and was eventually scrapped in 1935, not long after the merger between Cunard and White Star in

1934. When she was broken up by the ship breakers Thomas Ward & Sons in Jarrow the interior was auctioned off in 4,456 lots. The White Swan Hotel in Alnwick bought much of the interior of the first class lounge and part of a staircase, which they then faithfully reconstructed to make a magnificent dining room.

The first class lounge on the *Olympic*.

John continued to work on White Star liners over the winter months of 1911/12. On each trip back to Dumfries Alice tried without success to persuade him not to go on another ship. Early in 1912 John decided that now that he was engaged to Mary, he would end his seafaring days once he was married, but there were two more trips that he had planned to undertake. One of these was of course on the *Titanic*, but before that he was signed on for a trip on Cunard's *Carmania* as bandmaster, for the first time. John was only 21 and with the *Carmania* being a class leading ship of the time this was a great honour. Along with her sister ship the *Caronia* these two ships became known affectionately as "the grand Dames of the Atlantic". The trip that John was employed to sail on was from Liverpool to the Mediterranean, visiting Gibraltar amongst other places. The *Carmania* departed from the landing stage in Liverpool in the second week of March 1912 and returned on 1st April.

One of the musicians under the leadership of John was a close friend from earlier voyages named Louis Cross who played bass viol. He recalled an occasion on the *Carmania* when John played a prank on a woman passenger who made out that she knew more about music than she actually did. She had asked John to play a request, something which he was always willing to do, of a particular classical piece that was very complicated to perform. Without any hesitation John obliged, winked, smiled, whispered instructions to his band and played, at the end of which the woman came up, thanked the band and left. The actual instruction given by John to his fellow musicians was to play some American ragtime music very slowly; the woman didn't notice! This typified the fun-loving but professional attitude that made John so popular. Another of the five musicians on board was William Huchings, a cellist from Shooters Hill, London, who described John as "a very good musician". In his notebook he had John's address written down as 35 Buccleuch Street, Dumfries which was the home of John's fiancée Mary. Although they were not close friends, this wasn't the first time they had sailed together. William had applied to join the *Titanic*, but was deemed not up to the standard required. After the sinking William's mother made him give up playing on liners; he had a long career playing the cello and lived into his nineties.

John (first left) and William Hutchings (first right) as musicians on board the *Carmania*. As musicians their uniforms carried a lyre emblem on their left sleeve and cap.

The *Carmania* was built by John Brown & Co. of Clydebank and was launched on 21st February 1905 by Lady Blythswood, the wife of a former aide to Queen Victoria. The ship was powered by three steam turbines driving three propellers, a method of propulsion that was invented by Sir Charles Parson. This created a lot of interest because at the time it was reported that she was to be the forerunner of the much larger steam turbine ships, the *Lusitania* and the *Mauretania* . Her maiden voyage took place on 2nd December 1905 from Liverpool to New York via Queenstown. Several engineering experts on board were enthusiastic at how smooth and efficiently the turbines performed. The ship was 650 feet long with a beam of just less than 73 feet and a gross tonnage of 19,524. Passenger capacities were 300 first class, 350 second class, and 2,000 thirrd class. The *Carmania* continued to operate on the Liverpool to New York route without any major incident for several years, but in June 1910 while docked in Liverpool suffered a fire. Although the passenger accommodation was considerably damaged the main structure and machinery were unaffected. However, it wasn't until the 4th October that she returned to service with the repairs complete. On a trip from New York to Liverpool in October of 1913 the *Carmania* received an SOS call from the Canadian Northern Steamship *Volturno* which was travelling from Rotterdam to the USA, carrying immigrants and a cargo of barium oxide. During a fierce storm the barium oxide broke loose and caused a fire. Under Captain Barr the *Carmania* reached the stricken *Volturno*, but because of the severe weather had to stand by until the following day, when along with several smaller vessels, she picked up survivors. In all, 103 passengers and 30 of the crew of the *Volturno* perished. Several members of the crew of the *Carmania* received gallantry awards for their efforts in the rescue. During the First World War; the ship was converted to an armed merchant cruiser where she engaged the enemy a number of times and sank one German ship. In 1916 the *Carmania* was returned to Cunard and refitted to be used mainly as a troop carrier between Liverpool and Halifax, Nova Scotia. In 1920 the ship was reconfigured to accommodate 425 cabin class, 365 tourist class and 650 third class passengers. She stayed in service until becoming outdated and was eventually scrapped in 1932 after being sold to Hughes Bocklow and Co. of Blyth.

RMS *Carmania*, Cunard Line.

The Musicians

Being a musician on a ship in the early 20th century was not unlike being one in the early 21st century with cramped living conditions, poor pay and very long hours. In late December 1911 this was made worse when a Liverpool music agency, C.W. and F. N. Black (in July 1911 the agency was being run by Charles William Black but by the September he had been joined by his brother), operating from its third floor office at 14 Castle Street, Liverpool, struck an exclusive deal with all British shipping lines to provide musicians for their ships. The Amalgamated Musicians' Unions were concerned the musicians would be exploited, a concern that was proved to be correct. Black Brothers' office was just a few

Liverpool, The Liver Building, the Cunard offices, and the Harbour Office.

minutes walk from the docks and a matter of yards from the Cunard offices in Water Street, Liverpool. Prior to the Black Brothers deal, all musicians were signed on each voyage as crew and were paid the union agreed wage of £6.10s a month, plus an extra uniform allowance of 10s. They were also allowed an equal share of the collections (tips) from the passengers. Following the deal the musicians' wages were cut to £4 a month with no uniform allowance and they were signed on as second class passengers, not crew. Furthermore, there was an additional clause (clause 4) in Black Brothers' agreement which stated: *No collections from passengers must be attempted in any shape whatever, nor is anything to be solicited in any way. However, a further clause regarding collections confused the matter: I [Musician's name] agree that all gratuities presented to the band, individually or collectively in which I may play during my engagement with Messrs. C.W. and F.N. Black, shall be divided into equal shares plus one. The bandmaster shall take two shares and the remaining members one each" Signed, (musician's name).*

The *Olympic* under tow.

Before the *Olympic* was due to leave Southampton on March 13th 1912, a delegation from the Musicians' Union met with White Star boss, Bruce Ismay. They put forward their objections about Black Brothers' treatment of the musicians to no avail. Ismay said that if they objected they would be carried as second class passengers. The five musicians signed on as passengers and when the ship reached New York on 20th March 1912, the disembarking musicians had to pass an examination and answer questions by officials and also had to produce $50 in cash to prove they weren't destitute, in the same way as immigrants did. The company paid this money which was then reclaimed by the White Star Line agents after the *Olympic* had sailed with her five bandsmen on board. Again they were booked as second class cabin passengers for the return journey to Southampton. After this the musicians decided to abide by the new rules and sign ships' articles which put them under the command of the ship's captain. Although now classed as passengers, they still had to live in the cramped crew quarters, but because of this received an additional one shilling per month. This contracting out of musicians was to have far reaching consequences for the families after the sinking of the *Titanic*. The musicians had no alternative but to sign to these demands; if they declined they couldn't be signed on to play and the uniform they had bought would be of no use. One positive thing to come out of the *Titanic* tragedy was that it highlighted the shoddy treatment of ocean-going musicians. From 1st September 1912 the musicians' union took back control and it was decided to revert back to £6 10s for a 30 day month, plus 10s per month uniform allowance. The one condition was that the musicians had to be a member of the Amalgamated Musicians Union.

The
HEROIC MUSICIANS OF THE TITANIC
who died at their posts like men ~ April 15th 1912
G·KRINS Violin
W·HARTLEY
BANDMASTER
R·BRICOUX 'Cello
W·T·BRAILEY·Piano
J·W·WOODWARD·'Cello
P·C·TAYLOR·Piano
Nearer, my God, to Thee.
Or if on joyful wing cleaving the sky,
Sun, moon and stars forgot, upwards I fly,
Still all my song shall be,
Nearer, my GOD, to Thee, nearer to Thee.
"Nature might stand up,
And say to all the world,
This was a man."
—Julius Cæsar
J·F·C·CLARKE·Bass
J·L·HUME Violin

It is possible that there were originally to be ten musicians onboard *'Titanic'*, as the accommodation set aside for them was two cabins, each sleeping five people. Both cabins were on E deck to the aft; one was on the starboard side next to an instrument store and the other was on the port side, in the glamorous setting next to the potato washer and store! As it turned out eight musicians were eventually engaged.

WALLACE HARTLEY (bandmaster & violin)

Wallace Henry Hartley was born on 2nd June 1878 to Albion and Elizabeth Hartley in the mill town of Colne in the east of Lancashire, near the border with Yorkshire. His sister, Mary Ellen, had been born the previous year. When Wallace was seven years old a brother, Ughtred Harold, was born, but he died when he was one. Around this time Elizabeth gave birth to another daughter, Elizabeth.

As a child, Wallace was a member of the choir at the Bethel Chapel, Colne, where his father was choirmaster and he also took up playing the violin. It was Albion who introduced and made popular *Nearer, My, God, to Thee.* at the Bethel Chapel. When Wallace left school he worked at the Craven & Union Bank in the town, until his family moved to Huddersfield, Yorkshire in 1895. He became a member of the Huddersfield Philharmonic Orchestra, and a few years later in 1903 joined the Bridlington Municipal Orchestra as first violin. At the time of his death he was engaged to Maria Robinson from Boston Spa, Yorkshire.

In 1909 he took his first job on the Cunard liner *Lucania* sailing to New York from Liverpool. His next engagement was on the luxurious *Lusitania*, as second violin. In the autumn of 1910 he was offered the ultimate post as bandmaster on the *Mauretania*. He stayed on the *Mauretania* until the return trip from Liverpool to New York, which arrived back in Liverpool on 8th April 1912. Black Brothers the told him he was being transferred to the *Titanic*, as bandmaster, which would be sailing from Southampton. At this time he was living at Sunnyside, West Park Street, Dewsbury.

After the sinking of the *Titanic* Wallace's body was recovered by the *Mackay-Bennett* and numbered as 224. He was identified immediately by a ship's telegram, even though it was addressed to 'Hotley, Bandmaster Titanic'. His body was returned to England aboard White Star's *Arabic* and then to his home town of Colne on 18th May. There was a huge funeral procession with some 30,000 people lining the streets. There is a memorial to him in Colne, a pedestal with a thirty inch bronze bust on the top, and on the front of his house in Dewsbury there is a blue plaque.

SS *Arabic*, White Star Line, Liverpool.

FRED CLARKE (bass viola)

John Frederick Preston Clarke was born in 1882. He was raised in Birkenhead on the Wirral Peninsula, the opposite side of the River Mersey from Liverpool. He had dark receding hair and was 30 years old when he died. This was the first time that he had gone to sea after being persuaded by Black Brothers that as the winter concert season had finished, there would be fewer opportunities for work until the summer season began.

Clarke played the bass viola in the orchestra at the Argyle Theatre in Birkenhead and although he was not a member of the Philharmonic orchestra, he did play at the Philharmonic Hall on two occasions. Another venue he was seen to play in was the famous Kardomah Café in Church Street, Liverpool. He also had appeared at the Port Sunlight Coronation Concert in 1902 to celebrate the coronation of King Edward VII. He was well-known in musical circles and two weeks before sailing on the *Titanic* he attended a concert at the Argyle Theatre. A few days before leaving for Southampton he visited the theatre for a final time to say goodbye to his friends, and even joked that knowing his luck, after staying away from the sea for so long, he would probably go down with the ship. Clarke had hoped to gain a huge amount of experience from the trip and when he returned was looking forward to playing a season again at the Argyle Theatre.

When the *Mackay-Bennett* recovered his body, his personal effects were a diamond pin, gold watch, keys, knife, sovereign case, pocket book, memo book, 8s and a gold ring marked J.F.P.C., and he was wearing a crucifix. He was buried at the Catholic Mount Olivet Cemetery, Halifax, Nova Scotia, Canada, on 8th May 1912; his grave number is 202. On 10th May the Philharmonic Society held a benefit concert for his wife Ellen and sister. The Mansion House Fund of 1913 listed the Clarke family as Class F dependents, meaning they were entitled to fifteen shillings per week for his wife Ellen and three shillings per week for his sister.

PERCY TAYLOR (piano)

Percy Cornelius Taylor was born around 1880, which made him about 32 years old. He was married to an actress at the time of the sinking. Taylor had thinning dark hair and sported a very distinguished handlebar moustache. He was well known in London music circles as he was skilled on both the cello and piano. His address was 9 Fentiman Road, Clapham, Southwest London. After the sinking, his widow enlisted the help of the Musicians' Union as she hadn't received assistance from any *Titanic* relief fund. Eventually she, along with the other bandsmen's families, received help from various funds. His body was not recovered after the tragedy.

***Titanic*, shortly after launching.**

JOHN WOODWARD (cello)

John Wesley Woodward was born on 11th September 1879 at 24 Hawkes Lane, Hilltop, West Bromwich in the West Midlands, the youngest child of Joseph and Matha. He had six brothers and two sisters. His father was manager of the nearby Holloware Iron Foundry. The family were Baptist and as a young boy, John attended the Wesley Sunday School. His family later moved to 2 The Firs, Windmill Road, Headington, a suburb of Oxford. As an adult he was a man of a striking appearance, having dark hair and a fine handlebar moustache. He was 30 years old when he died.

Titanic **being fitted out in dry dock, the modifications to her promenade deck have yet to be made.**

After making a name for himself as a fine cellist by playing in several local orchestras and string ensembles, he left Oxford to join the Eastbourne Municipal Orchestra, on the south coast. Shortly afterwards he joined the Von Leer Orchestra at the town's Grand Hotel. His next position was with the Duke of Devonshire Orchestra. He continued to earn praise, not only as a soloist or member of an orchestra, but also as a teacher of the cello. This last position fell through shortly after he joined the orchestra.

The lure of playing on the world's most luxurious ocean liners, coupled with his keen interest in engineering, proved too much and in 1909 he took his first post with White Star Line, sailing to Jamaica and the Caribbean. He made several transatlantic crossings and some to the Mediterranean; it was said that he enjoyed the crossings to New York for the sheer glamour of setting foot on American soil. On 20th September 1911, he was on board the *Olympic* with John, when she collided with HMS *Hawke* in the Solent near the Isle of Wight.

In the winter of 1911 he played on Cunard's *Caronia*. It had always been his intention to resume playing in land-based orchestras, with the *Titanic* quite possibly being his last intended voyage as he was scheduled to play at the May dinner in Magdalen College Oxford.

His family were also listed as F Class dependents in the Mansion House Fund of 1913 and at the time of the sinking, he was engaged to a lady from London. There is a small brass plaque in All Saints Church, Lime Walk, Headington, dedicated to him, while in Eastbourne there is a triple panel brass plaque set into marble opposite the central bandstand. One section shows the *Titanic* sinking, the middle one an image of Woodward and the third an inscription. After the sinking his body was never recovered.

The modification to enclose the forward half of the promenade deck complete, and with smoke issuing from her three genuine funnels in preparation for her sea trials on the 1st of April.

THE TRIO

The trio consisted of Theodore Brailey, Georges Krins and Roger Bricoux . Having the Belgian and Frenchman together gave a continental feel to the music, with Brailey making up the trio having just completed a voyage with them.

GEORGES KRINS (violin)

Georges Alexandre Krins was born on 18th March 1889 in Paris to Belgian parents. In 1890 the family moved back to Spa in Belgium where Georges' father opened a drapers shop. Georges first studied music at the Academie de Musique de Spa and in 1902, he attended the Conservatoire Royal de Liege where he won first prize for violin with the highest distinction when he completed his studies in 1908.

He then worked for a short time in the family drapery before getting a position in Spa's La Grande Symphonie. In 1910 he played for a while at Trianon Lyrique in Paris, before moving on to the Ritz Hotel in London as first violin. Whilst working there he was living at 10 Villa Road, Brixton, only a short journey to the Ritz. He stayed until March 1912, when he was contacted by Black Brothers agency with a view to playing on the *Titanic*, which would have been considered an honour. The first trip that he took was on the *Carpathia* to New York. Following the sinking his body, if found, was never identified. Georges' name was inscribed on the family tombstone in Spa Cemetery and reads: *En memoire de Georges Krins mort sur le Titanic en 1912* (In memory of Georges Krins who died on the *Titanic* in 1912).

A few weeks after the sinking, a fund was launched for a memorial to the 'Belgian hero' but the fundraising was very slow between then and the outbreak of the First World War World. From this time Krins was forgotten and it wasn't until two Belgian *Titanic* enthusiasts took up the case in 2002, ninety years after the disaster, that a plaque was finally unveiled. It was placed on the front of Hotel Cardinal at 21 Place Royale, Spa, the site of the Krins family home from June 1910 to January 1911. The plaque was inaugurated on 14th September 2002.

George Krins' memorial, Spa, Belgium.

ROGER BRICOUX (cello)

Roger Marie Bricoux was the youngest of the *Titanic* musicians, having been born on 1st June 1891. At the time of his birth the family were living at Rue de Donzy in Cosne-Sur-Loire in France, some 70 miles south of Paris. At the time of the *Titanic* sinking he was living at 5 Place du lion d'or Lille, situated near the Belgian border and approximately 40 miles from Calais. Prior to the *Titanic*, he had worked on the Cunarders *Mauretania* and *Carpathia*. It was while playing on the ship on 17th March 1912 that he wrote to his parents on *Carpathia* headed paper, telling them that he was transferring to the *Titanic* for her maiden voyage. The last westbound Atlantic crossing he undertook was on the *Carpathia*, from Liverpool to New York, arriving on 2nd April 1912. He was accompanied on this trip by Brailey. After the sinking his body, if recovered, was never identified and rather strangely in 1913 the French

Roger Bricoux's memorial in Cosne–Sur-Loire. Translated right.

Roger Bricoux first prize of the Conservatoire du Monaco and cellist of the White Star Line liner *Titanic*. He was born on the 1st of June 1891, in the rue de Donzy, in Cosne-sur-Loire. He died at his post along with seven other musicians of the Orchestra on board.

This commemorative plaque was placed by the town of Cosne-sur-Loire and the l'Association Française du *Titanic* on the 2 November 2000. Following the judgement delivered by the family tribunal chamber of Nevers of the 11 August 2000 that the party involved, 'a member of the crew of the *Titanic* had died at sea during the night of the 14 and 15 of April 1912'.

army regarded him as a deserter and it wasn't until 2000 that he was officially registered as dead. This was thanks to the French *Titanic* Society, in particular Mr Marcel Van Nieuwenberg, that a judgement was rendered that he was in fact dead. On 2nd November 2000 a memorial plaque was unveiled in Cosne-Sur-Loire.

THEODORE BRAILEY (piano)

William Theodore Ronald Brailey was born in 1888 and was 24 years old when the *Titanic* sank. A dashing upright man with dark hair, he spent two years working and playing at Southport Pier Pavilion, Lancashire. Southport is situated approximately 20 miles north of Liverpool and was a very popular resort town in Victorian and Edwardian times. It still holds the famous Flower Show. Whilst living here, Theodore met and got engaged to a Miss Steinhilber of St Luke's Road in the town. He was also associated with Freshfield Aerodrome and was friends with Compton Paterson and Mr. J. Gaunt from the aerodrome.

***Top*: *Titanic* dressed in flags on the 4th of April for Good Friday the following day.**
***Above*: *Titanic* being manouvered prior to sailing on her maiden voyage.**

It is not known how many ships he served on. However, his last position prior to the *Titanic* was on the *Carpathia*, with Bricoux and probably Krins. Before leaving on the *Titanic* he was living at 71, Lancaster Road, Ladbroke Grove, West London. After the sinking, if his body was recovered it was never identified. There is no known memorial to him alone, but the musicians are commemorated jointly on various plaques around the country. In Southampton the original monument was unveiled on 19th April 1913 in the library. There was a mistake in the spelling of John Law Hume and it was spelt Hulme. The library, along with the memorial, was destroyed by bombing during the Second World War and it wasn't until 7th March 1990 that a replacement was unveiled, which now stands on the site of the former library. The original spelling of Hulme has been kept, despite comments from members of the public. The council felt that it was only proper to keep it the same as the original. As a family member, I disagree and think that it would have been an ideal opportunity to correct the error.

Memorial to the musicians in Southampton.

In Fred Clarke's home town of Liverpool there are two memorial plaques; one is in the Liverpool City Mission, Jubilee Drive, Edge Hill (this plaque was originally in the Beacon Hall, Wavertree Road, Edge Hill). This memorial has two mistakes! Hume is once again spelt Hulme, but more oddly, J. P. F. Clarke is put as J. F. C. Clarke. The other plaque is in the Philharmonic Hall, Hope Street, Liverpool. This memorial was originally situated in a corridor behind the stage, which meant that only the musicians and staff saw it. The hall was destroyed by fire on 5th July 1933 but luckily the plaque, although made from wood, was one of the few artefacts to escape unscathed. The new hall was opened in 1939 with the plaque once again sited behind the stage. It wasn't until 1995, during a major refurbishment that the plaque was moved to the foyer for all to see.

In Dewsbury, there is a tablet over the Churchwardens' pew at St. Mark's Church. The Institute of the National Orchestra Association had a plaque unveiled on 17th July 1912 by conductor Landon Ronald, who at the time was Principal of the Guildhall School of Music. In many countries around the world there are further plaques and memorials to the heroic bandsmen.

One of the many memorials to the the Titanic's musicians around the world. This one is in Broken Hill, New South Wales, a mining town on the edge of the outback. The four bands of the town were so moved by the story of the *Titanic*'s bandsmen that they raised funds for this memorial which was unveiled on the 21st December 1913.

Leaving Dumfries

On the Monday morning of 1st April 1912, as the *Carmania* was making her way through Liverpool Bay to the estuary of the River Mersey, across the Irish Sea in Belfast the *Titanic* was waiting to begin her sea trials. The previous Saturday she had taken on a crew mainly of officers, able seamen, firemen, engineers and boilermen for the trials which were to begin at 10am, when she left her dock on the River Lagan just off Queen's Island. Unfortunately because of a strong north-westerly wind it wasn't have been possible to navigate the narrow Victoria Channel and the trials were postponed until the following day. This, however, gave the crew members on board a day to take a close look at the giant ship. As the landing stage came into view, the sight of the two grand buildings that dominated the dock would have been both a welcome and familiar sight to John on returning from his several trips to the port. With the imposing Liver Building, on the left side, with its huge clock and Liver Bird

Liverpool, before the Cunard building.

statue looking out over the Mersey and the grand domed roof of the Port of Liverpool building to the right. The Cunard building that sits between these two today didn't start construction until 1914 and was completed in 1917.

Once he had disembarked from the *Carmania*, amid hundreds of fellow passengers and crew who were milling around the landing stage and dock buildings, he bid farewell to his fellow musicians. With John's keen sense of humour I'm sure he teased his friend and fellow musician Louis Cross about their next trips, John, of course on the *Titanic*, whereas Cross was to make the transatlantic voyage on the White Star ship the *Celtic*. The *Titanic* was due to arrive on the morning of April 17th and the *Celtic* due on 20th April in the evening, the day the *Titanic* was due to start the return journey to Southampton.

Lover's Walk, Dumfries.

John then made his way to Liverpool's Lime Street Station for the railway journey back to Dumfries. From the station John would walk the quarter mile along Lover's Walk, past the large sandstone bay fronted Victorian houses to the junction with Academy Street. He would turn left into Academy Street, pass the grand building of Dumfries Academy on his right, which was opposite no. 38 where his parents had first settled in the town. This would then take him past Greyfriars Church and the imposing statue of Robert Burns. Castle Street was just around the corner which passed by the north end of Buccleuch Street, within sight of the home of his fiancée, Mary. Just a few yards further, Castle Street joined George Street with John's home, no. 42 being right on the corner.

During the next week John spent time with Mary when she wasn't working and of course his family. Catherine in particular was delighted that her brother was at home. One thing that was of concern to Alice, John's stepmother, was the dreams that she had been having since John was on the *Olympic* when it collided with the *Hawke* the previous September. She feared that something was going to happen to John on the *Titanic* and tried to persuade him not to go, but with John being young and very single minded there was never any question that he would miss the trip, especially as it was to be his final voyage before marrying and settling down with his fiancée. Being a studious person, John also took every opportunity to hone his skills in readiness for the time when he would be playing in concert orchestras, now that he had advanced his ability on the liners.

On the morning of Monday 8th April 1912 John bid farewell to his family and fiancée Mary, probably with both of them unaware that Mary was carrying their child; he was never to set foot in Scotland again. He then retraced his walk of the previous week to Dumfries Station and boarded a train to Liverpool. After arriving at Lime Street, he made his way the short

Dumfries Station.

distance to the offices of Black Brothers, where he met with Wallace Hartley, Fred Clarke, Georges Krins, Theodore Brailey, and Roger Bricoux. The latter two and probably Krins, had arrived from New York a day or so earlier. They had disembarked from the *Carpathia* on 2nd April 1912 following a transatlantic crossing. Wallace Hartley had sailed on the *Mauretania*, which had left New York for Liverpool in the early hours of April 3rd and reached Liverpool on the 9th. After completing any formalities all six made their way to Southampton. John Woodward travelled from his family home in Headington, Oxford, while Percy Taylor journeyed from London. All eight would have stayed in Southampton that night in regular lodgings, as they were to board the *Titanic* all using the same boarding ticket no: 250654.

The following morning, Wednesday 10th April 1912, the crew members had been arriving at the docks from early morning, then making their way to berths 43-44. They must have looked in awe at the magnificent ship they were about to serve on. Also making his way from his lodgings at 12 Onslow Road, Woolston in Southampton, within sight of the *Titanic* berth, was John's former school friend, Thomas Mullin. The crew would have had to be on board and ready for hours, as the entire boarding procedure of passengers and luggage to when the ship left took a mere two hours, unlike today when boarding is spread over four to five hours, albeit with safety drill, something unheard of in those days.

John and his fellow musicians arrived in plenty of time to find their second class accommodation, which was only a short distance from the entrance. There were two rooms set aside for the musicians, each sleeping up to five persons, both on E deck aft. The two rooms for John and the musicians, although second class, would have been comparable to earlier ships' first class, with one big difference; there was only cold running water. The basin was a fold out that was housed in a mahogany cabinet that also had a vanity mirror, so when not in use it was simply folded away to make more space in the relatively cramped surroundings. To afford a limited amount of privacy, each bunk had a curtain that pulled across. There was however, unlike first class, no bath tub; for this the public bathrooms, situated at several locations throughout the second class cabin area, were used.

By 9.30am the second and third class passengers had began arriving in time to begin boarding at 10am. They boarded by the second class entrance, which was located aft on E deck. The first class boat train arrived from London's Waterloo Station at 11.30am, just 30 minutes before sailing, carrying the cream of society. By this time there were mountains of luggage stacked up by the ship; the Edwardians certainly didn't travel light! For the band there was no time for practice. However, all the men would have been familiar with the White Star music, having served with the company on previous trips. For this maiden voyage White Star had demanded Black Brothers secure the services of the very best musicians on their books. This they did, as all the men were well respected within musical circles both on land and at sea. They split into two groups, the quintet and the trio. The quintet comprising of Hartley, Hume, Clarke, Taylor and Woodward positioned themselves at the bottom of the grand staircase on B deck, near the first class entrance and began playing lively music, possibly American ragtime, to set a scene of joviality. The trio settled themselves in the first class lounge.

Prior to the sailing, the ship was teeming with passengers and visitors inspecting every inch of the ship, from the gymnasium to the grand staircase. This magnificent structure, situated between the first and second funnels, was the centrepiece of the ship and where the first class passengers, who read like a who's who of rich and powerful people, would meet in the reception room before dining. These included John Jacob Astor (and his pregnant second wife), Benjamin Guggenheim (the founder of Macy's department store), and Isidor Straus and his wife. Among the British were the Countess of Rothes and Sir Cosmo Duff-Gordon and his wife. On the landing of the staircase, halfway down, was a carved piece of two female figures entitled Honour and Glory Crowning Time, which flanked the famous ornate clock. The graceful curve of the stairs ended with a statue of a cherub holding an electric torch, above which was a stunning glass dome that let light cascade onto the surroundings below. Soon it was time for the visitors to leave and with the ship's railings lined with people and hundreds gathered on the quayside the *Titanic* began to gently leave her moorings at 12.15pm heading for the Solent, to the cheers and waving of all concerned. Even today there is something about an ocean liner leaving port that attracts hundreds of well- wishers and a flotilla of small craft.

Shortly after leaving her berth *Titanic's* suction and waves, created by her enormous propellers, nearly caused disaster. The SS *New York* was moored in tandem with the *Oceanic* at berth 38 when the suction created caused the *New York* to break free from her moorings and slide dangerously close to *Titanic*. Quick thinking on the part of the tugs *Vulcan* and

***Titanic* leaving Southampton.**

Hercules averted potential tragedy by tying her up to keep her in check until *Titanic* had passed. Although there are some claims that this delayed *Titanic* by about one hour, there is no evidence to suggest that it did.

Not long after this incident it was time for luncheon, with Wallace's quintet continuing to play by the bottom of the Grand Staircase. The first class dining room would soon fill up. During this time the ship was on her way across the English Channel to Cherbourg, a distance of some 80 nautical miles, to pick up more passengers. *Titanic* reached the port at 6.35pm, but as Cherbourg didn't have the facilities to accommodate the largest ships she dropped anchor just outside the harbour. The 274 passengers that embarked and the 27 that disembarked did so by means of the company tenders, *Nomadic* and *Traffic*. *Nomadic* could carry up to 1,000 first and second class passengers, while the smaller *Traffic* had a capacity of 500 in third class; she also had a conveyor to load and unload mail sacks. These tenders had been constructed in the same Harland and Wolff yard in Belfast as *Titanic*. Ninety five minutes later at 8.10pm *Titanic* raised anchor and set sail for Queenstown. She would have looked magnificent, fully illuminated sailing into the night. Of the embarking passengers 142 were first class, many of whom were Americans who had been touring Europe and beyond. These included the Astors, Margaret Brown (who was immortalised in the film *The Unsinkable Molly Brown*) and Colonel Archibald Gracie IV, a member of a wealthy family from New York State. There were also 102 third class passengers (mainly Europeans) looking to start a new life in America.

With the ship underway for the fifteen hour journey to Queenstown in the south of Ireland, it was time for the most important social event of the day, the evening banquet. The quintet was by now in full swing. playing tunes from White Star's extensive list, but at the same time remaining discreetly in the background. This would have created a convivial

Dumfries's bridges, the new bridge links Buccleuch Street and Galloway Street. The old Devorgilla Bridge was named after the mother of King John Balliol of Scotland.

Left: 5 Nith Place, where the Humes lived when John was born on 9th August 1890.

Above: Waterloo Place Congregational Church in the Whitesands, Dumfries. The family church not far from the family home in Nith Place. John's parents Andrew and Grace were active members of the church.

St. Michael Street School, not far from the Hume family home in Nith Place. It was here that John was schooled. Also at the school, although not in the same class, was Thomas Mullin, who became a steward in the Third Class section of the *Titanic*. A memorial to both men can be found in the hallway of the school.

One of the first trips that John made on a White Star line ship was aboard the RMS *Majestic.*

RMS *Baltic* of the White Star Line, one of the big four liners of that line. They were 'super liners' of their day and famous for their luxury and size rather than their speed. John's first taste of being a musician aboard these luxurious ships was aboard the *Baltic*'s sister ship *Celtic.* The other two sister vessels were *Cedric* and *Adriatic.*

SS *Mauretania*, the Olympic class ships of the White Star Line were a direct attempt to compete with Cunard's *Mauretania* and her sister *Lusitania*. Wallace Hartley's post before he was band master on the *Titanic*, was the same role on the *Mauretania*.

42 George Street Dumfries, the Hume family home at the time John was working as a musician on the liners.

Castle Street looking north from George Street. The Hume family home would have been behind the photographer.

June 1910 saw John playing as one of five musicians aboard the *Megantic* on her sailing between Liverpool and Montreal and back again.

Olympic on the left, *Titanic* on the right,
under construction in the Great Gantry, Belfast.

Launch of the *Olympic* 20th October 1910.

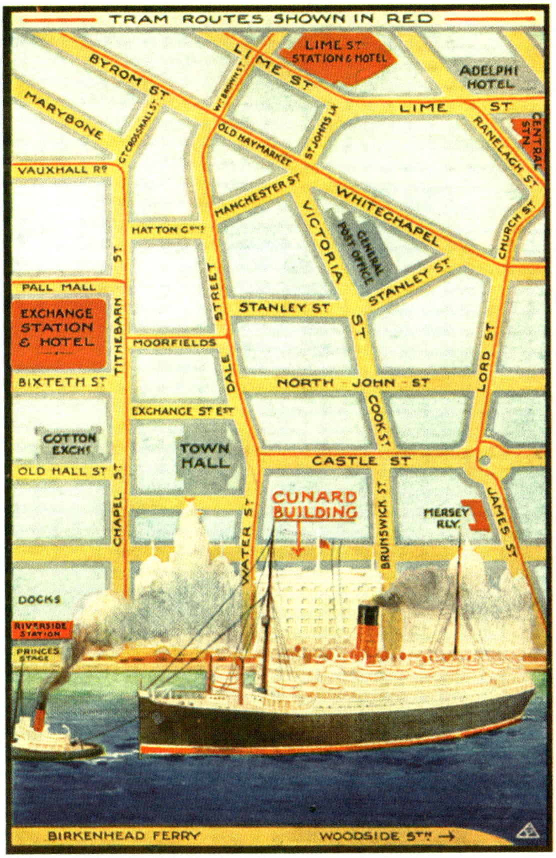

Until the launch of the *Titanic* the *Olympic* was the largest steamer in the world. Seen above she is passing the Ambrose Channel Lightship at the entrance to New York Harbour.

Street plan of Liverpool, Lime Street Station is at the top. and the Mersey with its landing stages at the bottom. Also of note is Castle Street running parallel to the river. It was in Castle Street that the Black Brothers music agency had their offices. The brothers had secured a deal with all the British shipping lines to supply musicians for ships.

The *Carmania* at the landing stages in Liverpool. In the background on the left can be seen the dome of the harbour offices.

Wallace Hartley's first job was on board the *Lucania* on one of its sailings between New York and Liverpool.

The White Star Wharf at Queenstown from which the tenders ferried passengers to and from the liners in the harbour.

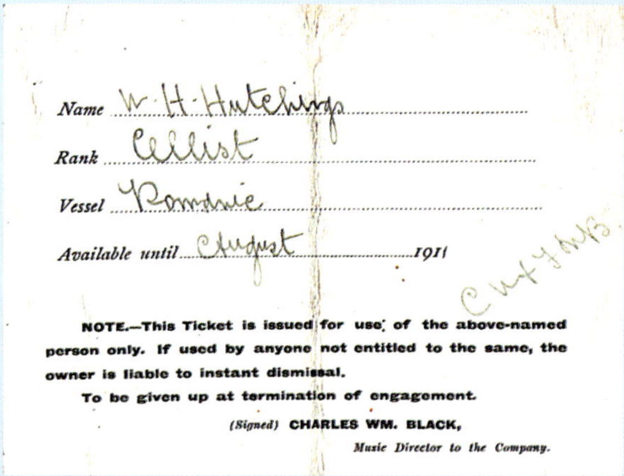

Name W. H. Hutchings

Rank Cellist

Vessel Romanic

Available until August 1911

NOTE.—This Ticket is issued for use of the above-named person only. If used by anyone not entitled to the same, the owner is liable to instant dismissal.

To be given up at termination of engagement.

(Signed) CHARLES WM. BLACK,

Music Director to the Company.

Right: William Hutching's, John's friend and fellow musician on the liners, at home in Shooters Hill London.

Above: William's crew pass for the *Romanic.* Prior to December 1911 all musicians were part of the part of the crew. After that date musicians were classed as passengers, a fact that caused their families considerable difficulty after the *Titanic* disaster.

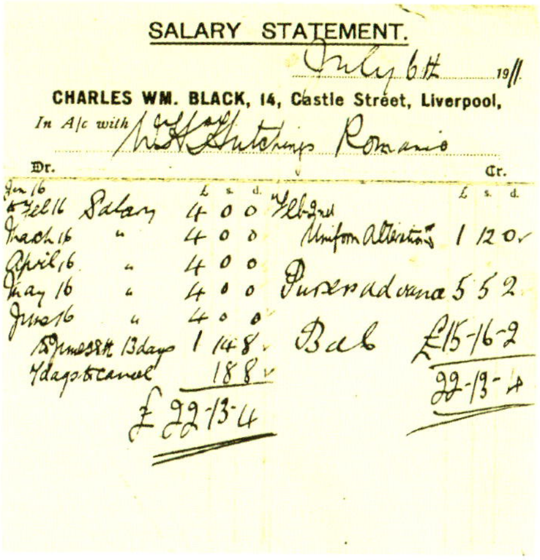

SALARY STATEMENT.

July 6th 1911

CHARLES WM. BLACK, 14, Castle Street, Liverpool,

In A/c with W. H. Hutchings Romanic

Dr.		£ s. d.	Cr.	£ s. d.
Jan 16 – Feb 16	Salary	4 0 0	Fld Fwd	
March 16	"	4 0 0	Uniform Alterations	1 12 0
April 16	"	4 0 0		
May 16	"	4 0 0	Purser advance	5 5 2
June 16	"	4 0 0		
	Dismissed 13 days	1 14 8	Bal	£15-16-2
	7 days to cancel	1 8 8		22-13-
		£22-13-4		

Above: William's wage slip from the *Romanic*.

Left and below: William's Continuous Certificate of Discharge a document that showed the career of a seaman, the ships and the capacity on board those ships in which the individual had served.

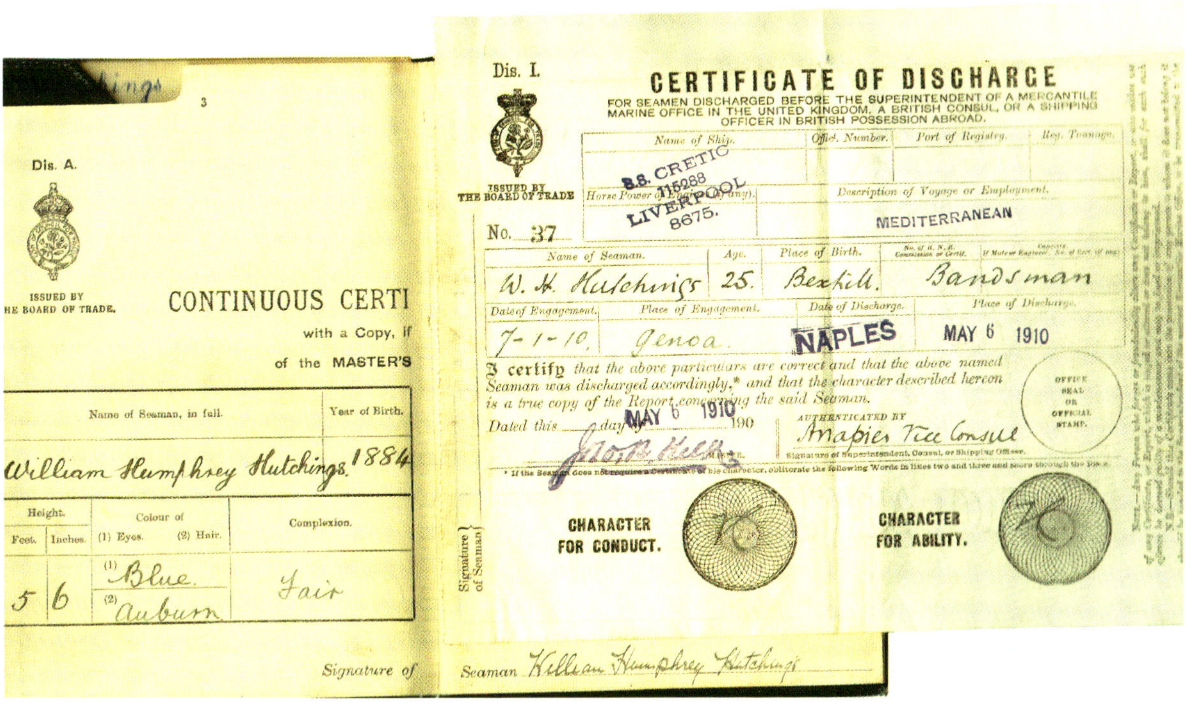

3

Dis. A.

ISSUED BY THE BOARD OF TRADE.

CONTINUOUS CERTI

with a Copy, if

of the MASTER'S

Name of Seaman, in full.	Year of Birth.
William Humphrey Hutchings	1884

Height. Feet.	Inches.	Colour of (1) Eyes. (2) Hair.	Complexion.
5	6	(1) Blue (2) auburn	Fair

Signature of Seaman William Humphrey Hutchings

Dis. I.

CERTIFICATE OF DISCHARGE

FOR SEAMEN DISCHARGED BEFORE THE SUPERINTENDENT OF A MERCANTILE MARINE OFFICE IN THE UNITED KINGDOM, A BRITISH CONSUL, OR A SHIPPING OFFICER IN BRITISH POSSESSION ABROAD.

ISSUED BY THE BOARD OF TRADE

No. 37

Name of Ship.	Official Number.	Port of Registry.	Reg. Tonnage.
S.S. CRETIC	115288	LIVERPOOL	8675.

Horse Power of Engines (if any).	Description of Voyage or Employment.
	MEDITERRANEAN

Name of Seaman.	Age.	Place of Birth.	Capacity.
W. H. Hutchings	25	Bexhill	Bandsman

Date of Engagement.	Place of Engagement.	Date of Discharge.	Place of Discharge.
7-1-10	Genoa	MAY 6 1910	NAPLES

I certify that the above particulars are correct and that the above named Seaman was discharged accordingly,* and that the character described hereon is a true copy of the Report concerning the said Seaman.

Dated this MAY 6 1910 day of 190

Master. AUTHENTICATED BY Naples Vice Consul

Signature of Superintendent, Consul, or Shipping Officer.

OFFICIAL SEAL OR OFFICIAL STAMP.

* If the Seaman does not require a Certificate of his character, obliterate the following words in lines two and three and score through the Dis. I.

CHARACTER FOR CONDUCT. VG

CHARACTER FOR ABILITY. VG

Signature of Seaman

The *Carpathia* was able to render assistance and sailed to the aid of the *Titanic*'s passengers. The *Titanic* struck her iceberg at 11.40pm., the ship sank at 2.20am. and it was 4.00am. before the crew of the *Carpathia* spotted the first of *Titanic*'s lifeboats.

The cable ship *Mackay-Bennett* was hired to search for bodies. She arrived at the location of the sinking five days after the *Titanic* had sunk. John's body was one of those recovered by the work of her crew and given the number 193.

The *Mackay Bennett* found so many bodies that she quickly ran out of supplies to cope. She sent a message to the Allan Line's SS *Sardinian* (above) saying that she was recovering bodies from the *Titanic* and to ask for as much canvas as possible to wrap or bury the bodies in. That evening the ships met and transferred the supplies.

John's posessions were returned to his family by way of the *Oceanic* on the 22nd of August 1912.

John's body could not be identified from the items that were found on his person. So his body had to be buried before he had been identified. He was buried along with 35 other victims of the disaster on the 3rd May. It was only later on the 16th of July that the identity of body 193 was established by matching the information that John's family had sent with the official photographs and descriptions of the victims.

The Sheriff Court in Buccleuch Street Dumfries.

Memorial to John Hume and Thomas Mullin in Dock Park Dumfries.

Detail from the memorial to the bandsmen of the *Titanic*, Broken Hill NSW.

The author and Millvina Dean the youngest and last surviving passenger of the *Titanic*.

atmosphere for the diners arriving, the ladies dressed in the finest gowns and adorned with fabulous jewels and the men sporting black evening suits. All through the meal the musicians would play, with the violins moving amongst the diners to play requests. This was a particular area in which John excelled as it only took a passenger to hum a few bars for him to pick up the tune and start playing. Violet Jessop, who had been on the *Olympic* with John at the time of the *Hawke* incident, thought that he was in fact the bandmaster, such was his confident manner and popularity with people.

During this time the trio of musicians were performing at their own 'venue', the reception area which was close to the A La Carte restaurant and the Café Parisien. The A La Carte was the last word in elegance, for this is where passengers could arrange private dinner parties. It was situated on B deck aft of the first class passageways. This restaurant was the brainchild of White Star for both *Olympic* and *Titanic*. The celebrated London restaurateur Luigi Gatti, who had restaurants in both London's Adelphi and Strand hotels, was to run it as a concession. Gatti bought with him his own staff for the voyage who were either French or Italian. Only one, French maître d' Paul Mauge, survived the sinking. The body of Gatti was recovered by the *Minia* and he is buried at Fairview Cemetery in Halifax. The Café Parisien was designed to replicate a European pavement café, being situated on part of the covered promenade and furnished with small groups of wicker tables and chairs. There were wicker screens on the walls separating some tables and the finishing touch was to have French waiters. Possibly the reasoning for Wallace Hartley to have French cellist Bricoux and Krins, who was from Belgium, along with Theodore Brailey on the piano, was to give the musicians a 'Continental' feel to complement the surroundings. Amonst those who used the Café Parisien were Major Archibald W. Butt and Colonel Archibald Gracie IV. Butt didn't survive the sinking. In Colonel Gracie's book *The Truth About The Titanic* which told of his and others survival, he spoke of how they listened to *the delightful music of the Titanic's band*.

As dawn broke *Titanic* was only a few hours from Queenstown (now called Cobh, pronounced Cove) its final port of call. At 11.30am the ship dropped anchor at Roches Point, the outer anchorage of Queenstown Harbour, from which tenders ferried passengers to and from the *Titanic*. The White Star tenders used that day were *America* and *Ireland*. In total 120 passengers embarked, of whom seven were second class and 113 third class. Seven passengers left the ship, having paid £4 for the journey from Southampton. Also taken on board were 1,385 sacks of mail. Along with the tenders, a number of smaller vessels also sailed out to *Titanic* to sell local crafts such as lace to the wealthy passengers. Disembarking were Father Francis Browne and the Odells with their two children Jack and Kate. Both Father Browne and the Odell children were keen photographers and they photographed some of the last known pictures of life on board and as they went ashore in the tenders.

At 1.30pm *Titanic* raised anchor for what was to be the final time to set sail for the open waters of the Atlantic. It was a perfect day of clear blue skies and what seemed endless visibility. On board there were 337 first class passengers, 271 second class, 712 third class and 908 crew. The crew would have numbered 909 but for one member deserting at Queenstown! As the ship began to slowly move from her anchorage Eugene Daly, a third class passenger, started to play *Erin's Lament* on his uilleann pipes (elbow pipes) for his fellow steerage passengers. Daly survived the sinking and lived in New York's Bronx until his death in 1966. The harbour pilot on that day was White Star's John Cotter. It was his job to guide *Titanic* from Queenstown Harbour to Red Bay at Crosshaven, just before the open water. He disembarked at around 2pm by climbing down a Jacobs's ladder from a gangway door on the starboard side and left in a small harbour craft. He was the last person to disembark before the ship hit the iceberg three days later.

Queenstown Harbour.

The Irish emigrants that embarked at Queenstown would now be settling into their accommodation in steerage. Although it was basic accommodation compared to first and even second class, it was better than many had been used to as it had electric light and heating. There were also proper beds, in the form of bunks, with spring and chain mattresses. Blankets and pillows were provided but not sheets. The cabins that were situated on the outside even sported portholes. Each cabin had its own wash basin filled via a cistern but no bath tub. In those days bathing was not considered a necessity as people had 'top to toe' washes at the basin. There were only two bathtubs in the whole of steerage, one for men and one for women!

Quite possibly the last people to see *Titanic* before the tragedy were a French trawler crew from Boulogne who claim to have seen the ship as it passed by them just off the south west coast of Ireland, later in the afternoon of 11th April. From the time *Titanic* left Queenstown to about the time of the near miss with the French fishermen, John and the rest of the musicians had some free time, from 1.30pm to 3.00pm. During this respite they would have practiced; this is borne out by some second class passengers who found the sound of the music coming from their cabins very agreeable. With John being very outgoing and sociable he would mix with other members of the crew, including stewardess Violet Jessop, who John had known from previous trips. She had always found him to be cheerful and with a smile for everybody. At 3.00pm the quintet assembled in the first class dining saloon for afternoon tea, while the trio made their way to the A La Carte restaurant's reception area. There they would play for the next hour, the music being a collection of light and jolly tunes. They would have had plenty to choose from as there were 352 of them in the White Star songbook. Each piece had to be learned and remembered as a number; White Star did not allow the use of sheet music.

In Edwardian times the music that was enjoyed ranged from full orchestral, operetta to waltzes and ragtime. On board there were no organised dances, but passengers spontaneously used to take to the floor. Such was the infectious nature of the music being played.

At 5pm the band would have their evening meal, which they had in the second class dining room located on D deck to the aft. The meal had to be over by 5.50pm to give themselves ten minutes to take up their usual positions in the reception area to the first class dining saloon and the A La Carte reception for the first class diners. They played for the diners until 7.30pm, during which time would stroll around the room serenading and taking requests. The final engagement of the evening was in the reception area where they would entertain with various pieces from the songbook and again take requests. This would have been more relaxed as the passengers were by this time full from the enormous menu which was complemented by fine wines and cognac. The evening would continue until around 11pm when the passengers would start to return to their cabins. The musicians would have relaxed with a cigarette before retiring to the cabins.

Queenstown from the docks.

The Iceberg

On the morning of Sunday 14th April the weather was slightly more overcast than the previous day. A morning service at 10.30am in the first class dining saloon was conducted by Captain Smith, with a similar service held in the second class dining room being presided over by the assistant purser Reginald Barker. These services lasted for thirty minutes and ended with the hymn *Oh God Our Help In Ages Past*; the naval hymn *Eternal Father, Strong To Save* was also sung, the latter with the poignant line *for those in peril on the sea*. The music for these two services was provided by the the quintet in first class and the trio in second. Mass was held in the second class lounge and was taken by Father Thomas Byles. Another was held in steerage afterwards.

The two operators in the wireless room, Jack Phillips and Harold Bride, were employees of Marconi. Strictly speaking they were not crew, although White Star paid their wages. They had been working through the night to repair the wireless system so they could send the backlog of telegrams. By the time the system was repaired both men were exhausted, but as they were the only two operators on board they had no choice but to continue. They had already received one message, sent from the Cunarder *Caronia* at 9am, warning of icebergs and field ice; this message was sent to the bridge. For most of the day though they were sending messages from passengers, who were impatient to have them sent to friends and family in New York. At 1.42pm the wireless office received a message from another White Star ship, *Baltic*, which was making its way from New York to Liverpool. the message said that a Greek ship, *Athinai*, had passed icebergs and large quantities of field ice at latitude 41 51 N and longitude 49 52 W. This message was delivered to Captain Smith while he was in conversation with Bruce Ismay who, it is alleged, put the piece of paper into his pocket. At 1.45pm Bride and Phillips overheard a message sent from the German ship *Amerika* to the US Hydrographic office in Washington DC. Maybe because it wasn't intended for *Titanic* it was never sent to the bridge.

During the day when the musicians had some free time John was speaking to Violet Jessop and told her that he was going to "give them a real tune, a Scotch tune to finish with". This wasn't his decision of course. Wallace Hartley decided on the order of the music. John may well have said this as a response to the comment of the violin being weak and that he would show them that the violin was certainly not weak! When it was 6pm and time for dinner, on what was to be the final evening, diners settled down to a banquet of ten courses. The menu in first class included oysters, consommé Olga, poached salmon, filet mignon lili, roast beef, roast squab (pigeon), waldorf pudding and chocolate vanilla éclairs. In second class the food was only slightly less elaborate including baked haddock and sharp sauce, curried chicken and rice, roast turkey, plum pudding and ice cream. In the second class dining room there was an early evening service taken by Reverend Ernest Carter, attended by about 100 people with the music provided by the trio. The weather that evening was described by second class passenger, Lawrence Beesley, as a beautiful starlit and moonless night with the sea resembling a mill pond. In the A La Carte restaurant Captain Smith was dining with Philadelphia financier George Widener and his wife Eleanor whilst being entertained by the trio of Brailey, Bricoux and Krins. At 7.30pm the *Californian* sent a message to the *Antillian* warning of large icebergs; the message was overheard by Bride and Phillips and this time it was taken to the bridge and handed to First Officer Murdoch. In the crow's nest were the two lookouts, Fred Fleet and Reginald Lee, although they had no binoculars to help them. At just after 7pm Murdoch had ordered the foreward forcastle hatch closed to stop the glow affecting the lookouts' vision, their task all the more difficult because of the lack of moon on the calm sea. At 9.40pm the ship received its last warning, from the Atlantic Transport Line ship *Mesaba*, but this never reached the bridge as Bride was getting some much-needed sleep and Phillips was inundated with passengers' messages to and from Cape Race.

Cape Race.

The evening's entertainment was described by passengers as a fine musical programme which included some Puccini and Dvorak, the evening coming to an end with *Tales Of Hoffman*, by Offenbach. The time was now around 11pm and passengers began to either return to their cabins or take a stroll on the promenade deck, although with the temperature now less than 33 degrees it wasn't long before most had returned to their accommodation. Some of the men from first class would have retired to the smoking room to enjoy a game of cards and a cognac. The musicians meanwhile had finished for the evening and were either going to bed or having a last cigarette of the day. High up in the crow's nest Fred Fleet and Reginald Lee were staring straight ahead onto the horizon, their eyes straining to cope with the cold, when Fleet noticed a large dark mass directly in front of the ship. Immediately he signalled to the bridge by ringing the small bell before picking up the telephone. Sixth Officer James Moody picked up the receiver and asked "what did you see?", "iceberg, right ahead" replied Fleet. Moody relayed the message to Murdoch who ordered the engines stopped while simultaneously instructing Quartermaster Robert Hitchens "hard-a-starboard" which had the effect of turning the ship to port. Murdoch then ordered "full speed astern", but the ship was still heading straight for the iceberg. Several seconds later the bow started to very slightly turn to port. The ship hit the iceberg with what appeared to be just a slight glancing blow, but with tons of ice cascading down onto the starboard well deck, which was the steerage recreation area. To all on the bridge it seemed like a major disaster had been averted. The time was 11.40pm. Down in steerage some of the passengers reported hearing a 'tremendous noise' as the ice ripped along the hull below the waterline, but in the first class saloon and accommodation the noise was nothing more than a slight grinding sound and judder. In the boiler rooms it was a different story as water was gushing through the gash in the hull, and on the bridge Murdoch ordered the closing of watertight emergency doors. Almost immediately after the ice crashed onto the ship some of the passengers from steerage appeared on deck and started to kicks lumps of ice around like footballs; it was a scene of almost unreal joviality after what had just happened. It wasn't long before passengers from first and second class also started to investigate, even claiming small pieces as keepsakes. Captain Smith was alerted by the juddering and went straight away to the bridge where he ordered the engines to be stopped. Just ten minutes after the collision water had started to pour into the mail room and lower steerage cabins. Captain Smith sent for Harland & Wolff managing director and chief designer Thomas Andrews, who then toured the damaged areas with Captain Smith to assess the damage. What they found were several holes in the hull over the length of 300 feet; these had been caused by the hull buckling and the rivets popping and not by one continuous 'slice' from the iceberg. The first five compartments had flooded. The ship was designed to float with three of the first five flooded or even the first four but no way could she float with the five flooded. With the bulkheads between compartment five and six only going up to E deck, when one flooded the water would spill over the top into the next one then the next. After making some calculations, Andrews told the Captain that there was no hope for the ship. At 12.05 am, just 25 minutes after the collision Captain Smith ordered Chief Officer Wilde to uncover the lifeboats, First Officer Murdoch to muster the passengers and Sixth Officer Moody to get out the list of lifeboat assignments. For Murdoch it would have been a grim task, knowing that there were only lifeboat places for half of the passengers.

Captain Smith.

Fourth Officer Boxhall was despatched to the quarters of Second and Third Officers Lightoller and Pitman. Captain Smith meanwhile went to the wireless room. Bride and Phillips seemed unaware of what had happened as they had been busy with passenger messages. It was only an hour before that the *Californian* had interrupted Phillips when he was in contact with Cape Race to warn of icebergs, but as he was so busy and exhausted he told the operator to "shut up; I am busy". Captain Smith told the operators: "We've struck an iceberg, you had better get ready to call for assistance". A few minutes passed and he at 12.15 am. returned and told Bride and Phillips to send the call for assistance. For many of the passengers it seemed like nothing had happened, but then more and more realised the ship had stopped and slowly people began to congregate by the Grand Staircase. Colonel Gracie said later that on his way to the foyer from his cabin he noticed that the ship had a slight list. It was around this time that Wallace Hartley had summoned his musicians to put on their uniforms and assemble in the first class lounge. For the first and only time all eight musicians were together. Only seven musicians would have had instruments because there was only one piano, unless Percy Taylor played a cello as he was skilled on both. John Carr of the *Celtic*, who had known Wallace and John from previous trips, said of Wallace: "Bandmaster Hartley was a man with the highest sense of duty. I don't suppose he waited to be called for but after finding out how serious the situation was, he probably called his men together and began playing. He often said that music was a better weapon for stopping disorder than anything on earth, he knew the value of the weapon he had and I think he proved his point".

As Violet Jessop was making her way to the deck she passed the band on their way to take up their positions. John smiled at her, although she said later that he looked pale, and he said " Just going to play them a tune to cheer things up a bit". It is reported that possibly it was the purser, Herbert McElroy, who ordered the band to play without interruption so as to avoid panic. During this time the crowd of people were either tapping their feet to the music or becoming restless and milling around. The music being played now was *Alexander's Ragtime Band* by Irving Berlin, which had only been published the previous year. The boat deck was a hive of activity, with the sixteen lifeboats being cleared ready to take on passengers. There were also four Engelhardt collapsible boats. In all the boats could only carry just fewer than 1,200 people. All the while passengers were being told to put on warm clothing and make their way to the boat deck. Some of the items people were taking with them showed the frame of mind they were in. Some filled their pockets with jewellery and watches, another carried a toy musical pig, while a theology student carried a bible. There were even some that asked the purser for their jewels that had been placed in the safe. On the boat deck the starboard side lifeboats, which were under the control of Officer Murdoch, had odd numbers. The port side even numbers were being controlled by Second Officer Lightoller. Lifeboat No. 6 was the first one to take on passengers, the order from Captain Smith being "put the women and children in the boats". This lifeboat was situated just by the entrance to the lounge where the band was playing, and Violet Jessop remembered hearing the music. As time passed and more boats left the stricken ship, Wallace instructed his men to move outside to a point near where lifeboat No. 6 had been. They would have had to collect their coats from their quarters and this may have been the time when some survivors had mistakenly thought they had permanently laid down their instruments and left their posts, but they had merely left them while going to fetch warmer clothing. This appears to have been confirmed by the accounts of two passengers, one of whom distinctly remembers them playing without lifejackets while another recalls seeing at least one playing with a lifejacket. Wallace together with John and Fred Clarke put on overcoats, with the latter two donning mufflers to keep out the cold. When they returned they took up their new positions, The cellists and Clarke, the bass violist, probably would have fetched chairs so as to be able to play. As there was no piano now Brailey would have given support to his colleagues.

Second class Swiss passenger Bertha Lehmann, who could only speak French and German, luckily met Roger Bricoux as he was returning to the deck with his coat. She asked him what was happening and was told to fetch her coat as all passengers were transferring to another steamer. He then helped her on with her lifejacket and escorted her to the boat deck and to a lifeboat. In the wireless room, Bride and Phillips were constantly sending the C.Q.D. signal to alert any other ships in the vicinity. The Cunard ship *Carpathia*, who was on her way from New York, picked up the distress call at 12.25am. By a stroke of luck although the wireless man had finished for the night he went back to verify some information and caught *Titanic's* call for help. *Carpathia* replied that she was on her way but she was 58 miles from *Titanic's* last-known position. Captain Rostron of *Carpathia* ordered all heating and hot water to be turned off so he could make as much speed as possible, which was seventeen knots. *Titanic's* sister ship *Olympic* also heard the transmission, but as she was 500 miles away, knew she would not be able to lend assistance.

The *Carpathia*.

Archibald Gracie, one of the last survivors to leave the ship told that he thought the band's choice of music, ragtime and cheerful tunes, was "a wise provision". This is the time that opinions start to differ with regards to the tunes played. Edwina Troutt, who was standing in close proximity to the band, said she heard *Land Of Hope And Glory* from Elgar's Pomp And Circumstance and at least one waltz, but could not put a name to it. First class steward, Edward Wheelton, remembers the band playing "selections from the opera and the latest popular melodies from England and America" although he couldn't identify any particular pieces. As the situation became more desperate, although opinions differed to song titles, one common opinion was that the music was not ragtime or such like, but more sombre and patriotic. Emma Schabert recalls one of the first hymns being *When We Meet Beyond*; another one, *Lead Kindly Heart,* was heard from a lifeboat. Some crewmen claim to have heard *Abide With Me* and *Eternal Father, Strong To Save.*

An hour after hitting the iceberg, Captain Smith ordered distress rockets to be fired and on the horizon could be seen the faint outline of a ship with lights flickering. Unknown to anyone on *Titanic,* this was the *Californian* that had sent an ice warning earlier. It was at this time, as the distress rockets were lighting up the decks, that passengers began to realise that the situation was fast deteriorating and a more concerted effort was made to fill the lifeboats.

As husbands helped their wives into the boats they reassured their loved ones by saying "look the band is playing and everyone is calm, there is nothing to worry about". At 12.55 am, when Margaret (Molly) Brown had been lowered in No. 6, as she was rowing away she could hear the band. Lifeboat No. 3 followed, after which No. 8 was lowered into the sea. At this time, the angle of the decks was increasing, but the men in the engine room remained at their posts to keep the power for the lighting and pumps. The lights could be seen from the lifeboats and the music could still be heard, with many claiming it still to be cheery. The biggest controversy as to the last music played came with Harold Bride saying that as he passed the band, he heard them playing *Autumn*, but in later years it was generally accepted that what he had heard was *Songe D'Automme*. The band, according to second class passenger Florence Ware, were still playing as she boarded the lifeboat at 1.30am.

By now the steerage passengers were making their way up to the deck, although many were confused as they spoke little or no English. Passengers still on board were now starting to panic in an effort to leave the ship, a crowd of people from steerage, Italians according to Fifth Officer Lowe's testimony to the commission, started to rush lifeboat No. 14. Lowe fired three warning shots. Hugh Woolner stated that he saw two flashes from a pistol that was fired by, he thought, First Officer Murdoch to stop a stampede on collapsible lifeboat C. This was the lifeboat that Bruce Ismay left on. By now it was getting to the stage of *'every man for himself'* , although many vilified Ismay for saving himself while hundreds of women and children died. With the ship starting to slip beneath the surface, the lights began to disappear, but passengers still remembered hearing music coming from nearer the stern. Collapsible lifeboat D was the last to leave and now men were starting to jump off the ship. Californian, George Broden, said when interviewed for the book *The Wreck And Sinking Of The Titanic* , that when he jumped at 2.05 am the band were still playing. With all boats and hope gone, Captain Smith released Phillips from the wireless room. Benjamin Guggenheim refused to don a lifejacket as he was dressed in his evening attire and was heard to say

Collapsible lifeboat D approaching the *Carpathia*.

"we've dressed up in our best and are prepared to go down like gentlemen". He gave a message to a steward saying that "If anything should happen to me, tell my wife in New York that I've done my best in doing my duty". The steward was saved and duly delivered the message. Now with the end fast approaching and with the deck at an angle of some 45 degrees, those still on board were struggling to make their way to the poop deck, while other were jumping into the sea. Before the final plunge Edwina Troutt told of hearing the band striking up *Nearer My God To Thee*. This was backed up by a steward, Jacob Gibbons, who said the sounds of the screams and the strains of the music would live with him forever. It would have been impossible for the band to continue beyond this point because of the angle of the deck, but somehow Wallace Hartley managed to strap his violin to his back before he and the others took to the water. The legend of *Nearer My God To Thee* being the final tune is, in my opinion, most likely to be true. Apart from it being heard by many people in the lifeboats, once when Wallace was asked by his friend Elwane Moody what he would play if a ship were sinking he replied: " I don't think I could do better than to play *Oh God Our Help In Ages Past* or *Nearer My God To Thee*". The latter was a favourite of his father, Albion, who was a choirmaster during Wallace's childhood.

Lifeboat alongside the *Carpathia*.

Harold Bride, after jumping into the sea, found himself under an upturned lifeboat and after freeing himself he saw the ship, "She was a beautiful sight, smoke and sparks were rushing out of her funnel, there must have been an explosion but we heard none, we only saw a stream of sparks. She didn't cause much suction when she went down". He added, "It was a terrible sight, men swimming and sinking". The ship finally disappeared from view at 2.20 am amid terrible crashing and screaming. Bride managed to climb onto the upturned boat, collapsible B, along with Archibald Gracie, Officer Lightoller, Jack Phillips and others. They spent the night franticly trying not to capsize and listening to the cries of men, women and children getting quieter and quieter as they drifted into unconsciousness before losing their fight for life. In sea temperatures such as these a person would not be expected to be able to survive more than fifteen minutes.

Carpathia reached the location given by *Titanic's* wireless operator at 3.30am but could see nothing. At 4.00am Captain Rostron ordered the engines to be stopped. All the crew and officers were now straining to catch a glimpse of something in the gloomy early morning light. Suddenly a crewman spotted the green light of a flare low in the water and realised that it was a lifeboat. A few moments later another lifeboat, No. 2, was spotted and under the command of Forth Officer Boxhall pulled alongside *Carpathia*. The first person was taken onboard at 4.10 am through the starboard gangway doors. As the stunned crew were informed that *Titanic* had sunk, other lifeboats started to appear and passengers were helped aboard, many in a state of shock, confusion or sobbing. Many of the women were no doubt thinking that their husbands had been picked up by other ships or were even on *Carpathia* already. The last survivors to be picked up were from lifeboat No. 12 which pulled alongside at 8.30 am. These included Harold Bride, Charles Lightoller and Archibald Gracie who themselves had been picked up from the upturned collapsible B by No. 12.

Captain Rostron now had the dilemma of where to head for; Halifax was the nearest port but there were reports of ice *en route*. It was decided that New York was the best option. Then followed the task of securing as many as possible of *Titanic's* lifeboats to the ships own davits; they managed thirteen. *Californian* had by now arrived on the scene and had started to search the area, but after one last scan of the surrounding sea Captain Rostron was satisfied that there were no more survivors and he set sail for New York at 8.50 am. At just after 8.00pm on Thursday 18th April, *Carpathia* was making her way past the Statue Of Liberty, with 10,000 people looking on from the Battery towards Pier 54 where a further 30,000 were standing in the rain. She would have looked a solemn sight with *Titanic's* lifeboats hanging from the davits as if at half mast. At 8.37 she unloaded the lifeboats and finally, at a little after 9.30am, the first of the 705 survivors began making their way down the gangplank. As *Carpathia* was making her way to New York, in Halifax, Nova Scotia White Star was organising the hiring of a ship to recover bodies from the site. The first ship to be hired was the cable ship *Mackay-Bennett*, owned by the Commercial Cable Company, at a rate of $550 US per day. She sailed from the wharf at 12.28 pm on Wednesday 17th April, with an all-volunteer crew under the command of Captain F.H. Lardner. On board was Canon Kenneth Cameron Hind of All Saint's Cathedral, Halifax and the chief embalmer of John Snow & Co., the largest undertaking firm in Nova Scotia. The ship also carried 100

Rescued passengers aboard the *Carpathia*.

simple wooden coffins, canvas body bags and several tons of ice. White Star had wanted to start recovery of bodies as quickly as possible, in the hope that they would still be grouped reasonably closely together. Progress to the area was hampered by fog on the Wednesday and Friday, but radio messages were sent to any ships that had seen wreckage or bodies. Two came back, from the German liners *Rhein* and *Bremen* reporting that there were bodies and wreckage floating in the sea. *Mackay-Bennett* arrived at the area on Saturday 20th April in the evening and prepared for the grim task of recovery the following morning.

At daybreak no one was prepared for the sight that greeted them. All around the sea was littered with wreckage and deckchairs with bodies bobbing about in the swell being kept afloat by their lifejackets. During the course of the first day 51 bodies were recovered, including a small boy aged about two. Those bodies that were too badly disfigured, or had no obvious means of identification, were buried at sea after a service by Canon Hind. This was after any personal effects, passports or such like had been removed, bagged and numbered, along with a description of the body for any possible identification later. The following day a further 27 were recovered, including J.J. Astor, who was identified by initials on his collar and by personal effects. It was concluded that because his body was badly crushed and covered in soot, that he had been killed by a falling funnel. Back in Halifax White Star had secured the use of another cable ship, the *Minia* to assist with the recovery; she set sail on Monday 22nd April.

It became apparent on Tuesday that there were far more bodies floating than *Mackay-Bennett* had supplies for. On Wednesday she sent a message to the Allan Line's *Sardinian* saying she was recovering bodies from *Titanic* and could she have as much canvas as could be spared to wrap or bury the victims in. Early that evening, the two ships met and lay alongside to enable *Mackay-Bennett* to take on the supplies. The search continued on Thursday with

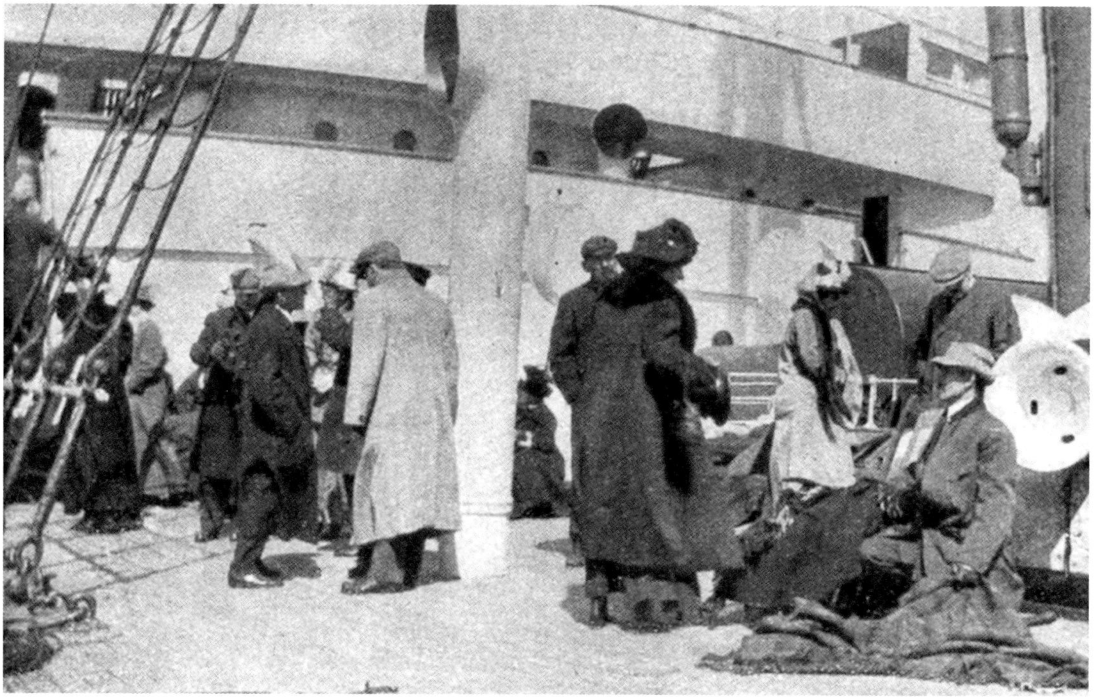

Rescued passengers aboard the *Carpathia*.

Harold Bride, needed to be carried ashore from the *Carpathia*, after the freezing water injured his feet.

nearly 100 being bought onboard. The bodies of John, Wallace Hartley and Fred Clarke had numbers quite close (193, 202 and 224) suggesting possibly that they were found near each other. Wallace still had his violin strapped to him when he was taken on board. However, this had mysteriously gone missing by the time his body was returned to England. Early on the morning of 26th April, *Minia*, who had reached the site late the previous vening, drew alongside and transferred more embalming fluid before *Mackay-Bennett* embarked on the return trip to Halifax. In all she had recovered the bodies of 306 people, 116 of whom were buried at sea. The remaining 190 were either in coffins or canvas bags.

Mackay-Bennett returned to Halifax at 9.30 am to the sight of flags at half mast and the sound of church bells tolling and docked at North Coaling Jetty No. 4. The quayside was lined with coffins and horse-drawn hearses ready to take the victims to the temporary mortuary, set up in the Mayflower Curling Rink in Agricola Street, where families came to claim and identify the bodies. *Minia* continued searching but only found another seventeen bodies, of which two were buried at sea. The others, including the body of Thomas Mullin, arrived in Halifax on 6th May. Two further ships chartered by White Star to search for bodies, the *Montgomery* and *Algerine* found only four bodies between them. *Algerine* returned on 7th June with just one, first class steward James McGrady of Southampton (body No. 330). It's strange that he was given this number as only 328 bodies are recorded as having been recovered. By this time any chance of significant numbers being found had gone because the bodies would have been caught up in the Gulf Stream and drifted for many miles.

From the time of the sinking to the last of the victims being bought ashore, newspapers around the world carried differing sensationalistic headlines, including stories of heroism and cowardice related by survivors. One story of a man dressing as a woman to get a place in a lifeboat was carried in several papers, with at least four men identified as that person. Over the days and weeks more information and facts were relayed to the media and this enabled reporting to be toned down.

Aftermath

As soon as the scale of the *Titanic* disaster started to unfold, plans began to be drawn up to launch funds to assist the victims' families, with the recently appointed Lord Mayor of London, Colonel Sir David Burnett, launching a public subscription headed by a Mansion House Fund. As virtually every corner of Britain had been affected by the sinking to some degree, other towns and cities across the country started to raise funds through similar subscriptions. Support was enormous and by 19th March 1913, less than a year after the sinking, the fund had raised £418,775, an incredible amount of money. Typifying the feeling across the country, a concert was held in London's Royal Albert Hall on the afternoon of 24th May 1912 (Empire Day). This was the setting for a remarkable spectacle in which all members of the seven main London orchestras combined to play as one, totalling more than 500 musicians, to honour the bandsmen who had perished. Newspapers called this "The greatest orchestra ever assembled". The conductors were Sir Edward Elgar, Sir Henry Wood, Percy Pitt, Landon Ronald, Thomas Beecham, Fritz Ernaldy and Dutch conductor Willem Mengelberg (who had travelled from Berlin especially for the occasion). The first piece played was Chopin's Funeral March, arranged and conducted by Sir Henry Wood, followed by Arthur Sullivan's *In Memoriam*, conducted by Percy Pitt. The Australian singer Ada Crossley sang Mendelssohn's *O Rest In The Lord*. Closing the event was the hymn, *Nearer My God to Thee*, which was conducted by Sir Henry Wood. After the first eight bars he turned to face the audience and conducted their singing to the hymn. The sight and sound of the voices of thousands coming as one, would have been majestic.

On the other side of the Atlantic the heroic acts of the bandsmen also found their way into the hearts of many people. Mrs Joseph Regneas, wife of the operatic voice teacher, held a musical concert in her home at 133 West 180th Street, New York on Saturday 27th April 1912, with elite members of New York society in attendance. Two weeks later, on 9th May, a concert was held at the Apollo Club in Brooklyn "In Aid Of the Musicians who perished by the sinking of the *Titanic*". The concert at the home of Mrs Regneas raised $1,000 and shortly after the concert a cheque was sent to Mr Arthur Foote in Brookline, Massachussets, who had been appointed head of the Boston *Titanic* Musicians Fund. Accompanying the cheque was a note from the donors saying "this is a tribute from the musicians of New York; to the memory of the band who kept playing in an effort to calm the passengers as the ship sank".

FUND FOR FAMILIES OF TITANIC BANDMEN

Relatives of Men Who Played as Ship Went Down Send Thanks to Musicians Here.

W. Theodore Brailey

John Law Hume

Mme. Joseph Regneas of 133 West 180th Street received yesterday the last of a series of letters from relatives of members of the steamship Titanic's band to whom Mme. Regneas sent a fund of $1,000 obtained through a concert which Mme. Regneas and several of her musical friends gave at Mme. Regneas's home in this city on April 27. With the money, the donors sent a message explaining that it was a tribute from musicians in this city to the memory of the men who kept on playing in an effort to calm the passengers on the Titanic as the great liner went down.

The letters received in acknowledgment of the fund expressed the deepest appreciation for the spirit which prompted sending it. Relatives of John Law Hume, known to his associates as "Happy Jock" Hume, and of W. T. Brailey, another of the Titanic's musicians, enclosed with their letters of thanks photographs of these two men, which are reproduced herewith.

Members of Mr. Hume's family have been manufacturers of musical instruments in Scotland for generations. He was educated for concert work but took a place in the Titanic's band for practice. The other members of the band in addition to Mr. Brailey and Mr. Hume were: W. Hattry, the bandmaster; P. C. Taylor, J. W. Woodward, R. Bricoux, James Clark, and George Krius.

***New York Times* article on the results of Mrs Joseph Regneas's concerts in aid of the bandmembers. Courtesy *New York Times*.**

In early July the donation was sent to the *Titanic* Relief Fund in Liverpool, with the proviso that it was only to be given to the immediate families of the bandsmen. Many of the relatives including the Humes sent letters of thanks, some accompanied by photographs, to the Regneas family. In the wake of the huge amount of sympathy and disbelief at the tragedy coming from every corner of the globe, it makes one particular act even harder to comprehend. On 30th April 1912, just fifteen days after the sinking, when John's body had just been recovered but still not identified, my great-grandfather, Andrew Hume, received a bill from Black Brothers for the amount of 5s. 4d, to cover an outstanding amount owed on John's uniform account that J. J. Raynor and Sons had forwarded to them. The letter arrived at my family's home on the same day that the *Mackay-Bennett* arrived back in Halifax with the recovered bodies. It must have been one of the most cold and heartless acts to emerge from the disaster. Black Brothers also completely washed their hands of responsibility to any claim by the families for financial assistance and said that the families should seek compensation from their (Black Brothers') insurers. However, the insurance company claimed that the musicians were working as independent contractors and were just using the Black Brothers' agency as their booking company. Still in shock, the families then approached the White Star Line to claim financial benefits under the Workmen's Compensation Act. The problem here was that as the men had been booked as second class passengers and not members of the crew, they weren't covered by the Act and therefore were not entitled to any benefits. The only avenue left was to go to court, with the matter heard at Liverpool County Court on 31st October 1912. Although the court was in agreement with the families, Judge Thomas had no alternative but to rule they were indeed working as independent contractors and therefore not covered by the Act. As a last ditch attempt, the Musicians' Union appealed to the White Star Line saying that "the men had performed a selfless act of heroism which resulted in their deaths". Unfortunately, they didn't relent. In a letter which appeared in an Irish newspaper in December 1912, Black Brother tried to exonerate themselves by stating that although the company were under no legal obligation "*the company have generously made ex-gratia payments to the amount of nearly £700*". It was also said by them "*£1,555 has been distributed from a fund organised by ourselves for the benefit of the relatives*". Whether or not this actually happened will probably never be known. They said that they wished to refute allegations in various newspapers that stated that the dependents of the musicians had been in any way badly treated. In my view, it would seem strange for the company to make these payments, especially after the way that John's family were treated just two weeks after the sinking. Also, there seems to be no record of any family acknowledging such payment. Furthermore, in the *Dumfries & Galloway Standard* there is no mention of Andrew ever receiving anything from Black Brothers, which would be rather strange, bearing in mind the enormous coverage of every aspect of the sinking and aftermath. In the end it was down to the *Titanic* Relief Fund, swelled by donations from the likes of the Regneas family, to save the day.

The realisation that John had been lost to the sea was starting to hit home, even though there was no official word. The fact that he wasn't on the list of survivors and the reports filtering through about the band having played on to the last, added to the confusion. On 17th April Andrew travelled down to the White Star offices in Liverpool, desperate to get any information that he could, but it was

But we believe the limit is reached in the case of the father of J. L. Hume, of Dumfries. On April 30th, just 15 days after the disaster, when the family of the late J. L. Hume were still mourning their loss, the following callous letter was sent to Hume's father:—

From C. W. & F. N. Black,
Head Office, 14, Castle Street,
Liverpool, April 30th, 1912.

Mr. A. Hume,
42, George Street,
Dumfries, N.B.

Dear Sir,—We shall be obliged if you will remit us the sum of 5s. 4d., which is owing to us as per enclosed statement. We shall also be obliged if you will settle the enclosed uniform account.—Yours faithfully,

(Signed) C. W. and F. N. BLACK.

The enclosed uniform account is as under:—

S.S. "Titanic," April 4th, 1912.

Received from Messrs. J. J. Rayner & Sons, the under-mentioned goods. I hereby authorise Messrs. C. W. & F. N. Black to deduct the sum as signed for from my wage account:—

	£	s.	d.
Tunic, new collar	0	2	6
,, cleaned and pressed	0	1	6
,, White Star buttons	0	1	0
Vest, new buttons 9d., cleaned and pressed 6d.	0	1	3
Trousers cleaned and pressed	0	1	0
Lyre, small	0	2	0
	£0	9	3

Signed JOHN HUME.

Witness S. B. YEOMANS.

Notice.—Please see that your goods correspond with this invoice.

Letter sent by Black Brothers to Andrew Hume.Courtesy Musicians' Union Archive, Stirling University.

a fruitless journey as information was very sketchy and contradictory. In the Costin household Mary was hoping against hope that John would return, but as the days went by the hope turned to grief. The following week Andrew was advised to contact the White Star offices in Southampton and was asked to send a photograph and detailed description of his son to help with identification. Andrew wasted no time in sending the information and a photograph of John. This was then sent to White Star's New York offices at 9 Broadway.

At the temporary morgue for the unidentified bodies at the Mayflower Curling Club in Halifax items they carried were photographed and numbered, and their personal effects were itemised, bagged and then listed with the same number. The photograph of John's body, along with many others, was sent to the New York office by the Deputy Provincial Secretary for Nova Scotia, Mr Fred F Mathers. The description that accompanied the photograph was:

No. 193

Male: *5ft 9in* ***Weight:*** *145lbs* ***Age:*** *about 28* ***Hair:*** *Light curly, clean shaven* ***Marks:*** *None Buried at Fairview Cemetery Halifax NS* ***Wore:*** *Light rain coat: Uniform jacket with green facing and vest: Purple muffler* ***Carried:*** *Cigarette case, silver watch, knife with carved pearl handle, brass button marked African Royal Mail and an English lever watch.*

Fairview Cemetery, *Titanic* section.

Due to the number of unidentified bodies, the authorities had to start arranging burials and on 3rd May John, along with 35 other victims, was buried at the non-denominational Fairview Lawn Cemetery, his grave being identified just by the number 193. After the burials, then began the painstaking and harrowing task of matching descriptions and photographs sent by loved ones. Together with the information from Canada, gradually names were put to the victims. Eventually, on 16th July 1912 White Star employee, Harold Wingate of the New York offices, sent proof to Halifax "that they have been able to identify No. 193 as John Law Hume, a bandsman of the *Titanic*". Unlike bandleader, Wallace Hartley, who was identified by his belongings and sent home to England to be laid to rest, John had already been buried and so couldn't be returned to his native Scotland. Also buried at Fairview is Thomas Mullin (in grave No. 323), John's colleague from school; his body was one of the last to be recovered by the *Minia*.

On August 9th 1912 White Star's Mr Wingate notified Mr Mathers in Halifax that John's personal effects (listed as carried) were going to England aboard White Star's *Oceanic*, which also had been built at Harland and Wolff's Belfast yard. *Oceanic* was launched 14th January 1899 and undertook her maiden voyage on 6th September that year from Liverpool via Queenstown to New York. From her launch date until the completion of *Celtic* in 1901, she was the largest ship in the world, with a length of 704 feet and width of 63.8 feet and gross tonnage 17,272. *Oceanic* was a twin screw vessel that had a maximum speed of 19 knots. On 11th October 1905 after a trip from New York to Liverpool, over 30 of her stokers were arrested for refusing to work over pay and working conditions and were sentenced to one week's hard labour. During a transatlantic crossing on 13th May 1912, *Oceanic* came across one of the collapsible lifeboats from *Titanic*. with three bodies inside, which were buried at sea. The lifeboat was taken to New York.

Oceanic left New York bound for Liverpool on Tuesday 13th August and after the arduous journey from Halifax, via New York and Liverpool, the items duly arrived at 42 George Street, Dumfries on 22nd August 1912. The package was addressed to John's step-mother, Alice Mary Hume. Annie Agnes Kellochan, who lived at 37 Queen Street and had been a friend of Alice from when she was running her shop in nearby Nith Place, witnessed the signature on the receipt, which was then returned to Mr Mathers in Halifax via the White Star offices in Liverpool.

The grief that the family felt was almost too much to bear, especially Kate, as she had been very close to her brother. These feelings of loss were felt equally in the Costin household, perhaps even more so as Mary was cut off completely from the family who had been to become her in-laws. When Mary asked Andrew for financial help for when her child was born she was told, in no uncertain terms, that John had no estate for Mary to claim on.

In a letter to Mary on 26th June Andrew wrote "apart from some clothes and letters the only estate my son left was his debt standing to me, which during the past year he had started to pay off". There was no compassion for the fact that she was carrying John's child and Andrew refused to admit that John was the father, even saying that he had a letter from John denying the fact. One can imagine what it was like for Mary, 21 years old, her father having died when she was four and being pregnant whilst still single. Undeterred, Mary was aware of the Boston Musicians donation to the families and pressed Andrew for some financial help. Eventually it was agreed that she would receive a cheque, which was deposited into the Commercial Bank of Scotland with Mr Sinclair, the manager, acting as the agent. Mary did not believe this was the total sum that she would receive, but as her child hadn't been born yet there was little else she could do. Andrew was adamant that he was going to do no more to help. Fortunately, Mary's mother, Susan, was the office keeper at Walker and Sharpe, a firm of solicitors in Maxwelltown where a Mr G T Hendrie worked and when he learned of Mary's plight, he offered his assistance.

On 28th June 1912 Mary, with the help of Mr Hendrie, lodged an application with the Relief Fund in Liverpool for a grant to help. In reply she was told to contact the committee again once her baby had been born and if they were satisfied that John was the father, her application would be considered. Mary wasted no time in telling Andrew of her intentions regarding the Liverpool fund. The ensuing months would have been extremely difficult for her, and indeed the rest of her family, as she tried to cope with not only the alienation, but the sense of loss. On Friday 18th October 1912 Mary gave birth to a baby girl who she named Johnann Law Hume. Unfortunately, as John was dead and therefore couldn't confirm or contest that he was the father, Mary had no alternative but to put the child as illegitimate on the birth certificate. However, before she could receive any money, Mary had to convince the Sheriff, plus satisfy the fund committee, that John was the father. To prove this the case had to go before the Sheriff Court at 40 Buccleuch Street, Dumfries, directly opposite the Costin home at 35 Buccleuch Street. The case was heard on 3rd December 1912 before Sheriff Campion and a decree was granted that John was the father, which was then filed by the Register for Corrected Entries on the birth registry. It was also decreed that Mary was to receive £67 2s from the Relief Fund. Andrew was aware of the hearing and was invited to attend, but chose not to, although he was informed of the outcome. With this proof from the court, Mary was now eligible for financial help for herself and her daughter. Mr Hendrie,

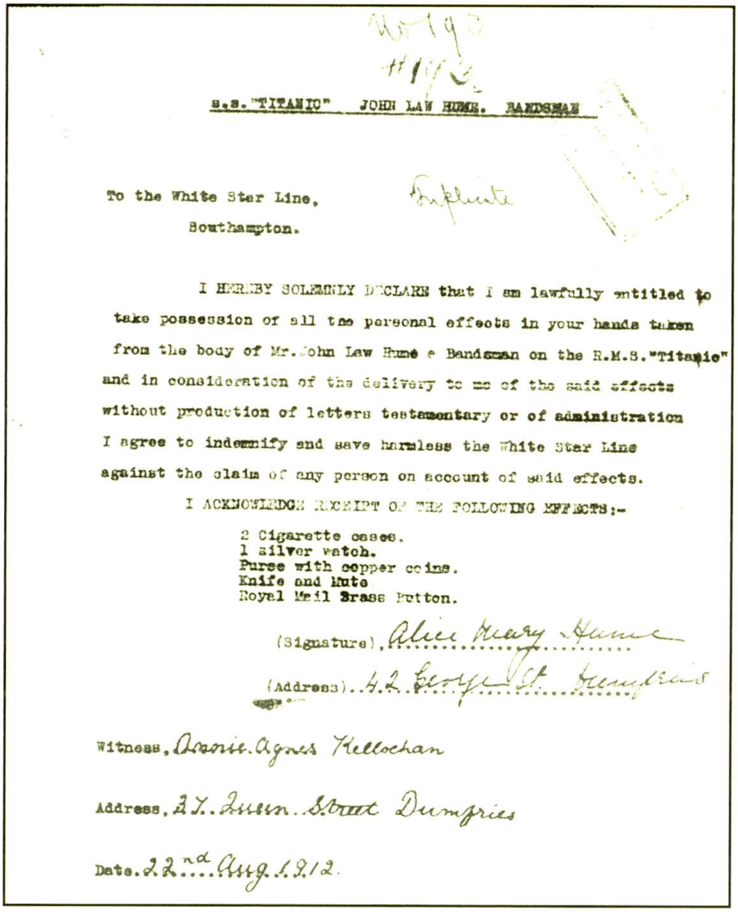

s.s. "TITANIC" JOHN LAW HUME. BANDSMAN

To the White Star Line,
Southampton.

Duplicate

I HEREBY SOLEMNLY DECLARE that I am lawfully entitled to take possession of all the personal effects in your hands taken from the body of Mr. John Law Hume a Bandsman on the R.M.S. "Titanic" and in consideration of the delivery to me of the said effects without production of letters testamentary or of administration I agree to indemnify and save harmless the White Star Line against the claim of any person on account of said effects.

I ACKNOWLEDGE RECEIPT OF THE FOLLOWING EFFECTS:-

2 Cigarette cases.
1 silver watch.
Purse with copper coins.
Knife and Mute
Royal Mail Brass Button.

(Signature). Alice Mary Hume

(Address). 42 George St Dumfries

Witness. Annie Agnes Kellochan

Address. 27. Queen. Street Dumfries

Date. 22nd Aug. 1912.

Receipt of John's personal effects signed by his stepmother Alice Mary Hume. Courtesy of Nova Scotia Archives and Record Management.

Mary's solicitor, duly sent a letter and a copy of the decree to the relief fund in Liverpool. Mary received a communication from Mr Percy Corkhill, the solicitor to the Corporation of Liverpool and in charge of the fund, confirming the amount that she would be awarded.

Unknown to Mary, Andrew had also applied for a grant from the same fund to try and recover the cost of violins that he valued at £325, which John had taken with him on the *Titanic* plus an amount of £400 to pay off a bond on his property that had been lent to John.

This application was rejected as it was deemed that he could not be classed as a dependant of his son. He knew that Mary had been granted an amount from the fund and on 14th November 1912 Andrew wrote to Mr Corkhill, "I am requested by my agents here, Messrs Henderson and Sons, to inform you that the claims presented by Mr Hendrie for the amount of £65 for aliment and £2 2s of involving expenses for an illegitimate female child, have now been fully settled and she has been paid more than this amount. Mr Hendrie now withdraws his claim. I consider that I, as his parent and legal representative, ought to have an opportunity of rectifying the alleged evil". Andrew had first sought the advice of Mr Henderson after Mary began pressing him for some money from the Boston Fund, before she had given birth.

It was made clear in reply by Mr Corkhill that Mary's claim was a good one and they fully believed that it was her and John's intention to marry on his return. They were satisfied too, that he was Johann's father. Confusion was caused when the committee were under the impression that the court's decree, regarding John as the father, was binding and that any payment Andrew received would be passed on to Mary. On 2nd January 1913 a cheque for £67 2s was received and in return Andrew sent a letter to the fund committee in Liverpool, acknowledging receipt of the money. Andrew had already received £25, £71 9s 7d and £140 from the Mansion House and Daily Telegraph funds before Johann was born. It wasn't until April, despite repeated requests by Mary for Andrew to pay her the money that was awarded to her, that Mr Hendrie, once again, took up the case. Andrew maintained that the money was to cover the cost for the amount he had already paid to Mary, as it was for the amount that was in his application. Confirmation was received on 24th April 1913 from Mr Neale, from the fund committee in Liverpool that the money was indeed sent to Andrew for the benefit of Mary and Johann. The following day Mr Hendrie contacted Andrew asking him for the money. It was met with a rather terse reply, stating that it was sent to him as a result of his own claim. He added that if it was sent to him to forward it on, he would have either have returned it to Liverpool, or sent it to Mary's solicitor.

As Andrew refused to co-operate, Mary was left with no alternative but to take the matter to the Sheriff Court. The case was heard on Thursday 19th June 1913, once again before Sheriff Campion. Andrew was represented this time by Mr I F Edgar of Whitelaw and Edgar and Mary by Mr Hendrie. Both of these legal firms still practise in Dumfries today under the same names. The court heard that Andrew had paid a sum into the Commercial Bank and that he had received money from the fund in Liverpool, but denied it was for Mary and Johann. As they couldn't reach agreement, the hearing was adjourned until Tuesday 2nd September 1913.

When the case returned, Sheriff Campion decided in favour of Mary and that Andrew should instruct his bank to raise a cheque for £67 2s. The Costin family hoped now that this traumatic period was over and that Mary could at last move on with her life in bringing up her daughter. Unfortunately, this wasn't the end of the matter. Andrew now claimed

But even assuming that a man does remain in the service, just compare the following statements of a bandsman's wages on the Royal Mail Steam Packet Company's ship, "Amazon." Before Messrs. Black provided the musicians, a bandsman received as follows (we quote from his wage-sheet of December 16th, 1911):—

	£ s. d.		£ s. d.
Wages:		Deductions;	
1 month, 20 days.........	10 16 8	Slops..........	1 17 6
Overtime.......	0 18 6	,, ...	0 3 0
	£11 15 2		£2 0 6
Deductions as per contra	2 0 6		
	£9 14 8		

Then there was 10s. a month towards uniform.

When Messrs. Black provided the musicians the bandsman's wage-sheet for April 29th, 1912, was as under:—

	£ s. d.		£ s. d.
March 6 to April 6	4 0 0	Uniform	2 14 6
April 6 to 27th, 22 days	2 18 8	Wine a/c	0 14 5
		Balance	3 9 9
	£6 18 8		£6 18 8

One might jump to the conclusion that the musicians at the higher rate were a superior class to those provided by Messrs. Black, but that is not the case, for the two wage-sheets shown above both belong to the same musician, and for services in the same ship.

As one may see, the wages have been reduced considerably, for with a longer period, under the new régime, the musicians' earnings have been reduced nearly 50 per cent.

Now while we admit that anyone who finds the musicians and the music for someone else is entitled to some recompense, we cannot for one moment agree that Messrs. Black or anyone else are entitled to anything like 50 per cent. of the fee allowed them for each bandsman.

Pre and post Black Brothers wage slips. Courtesy Musicians' Union Archive, Stirling University.

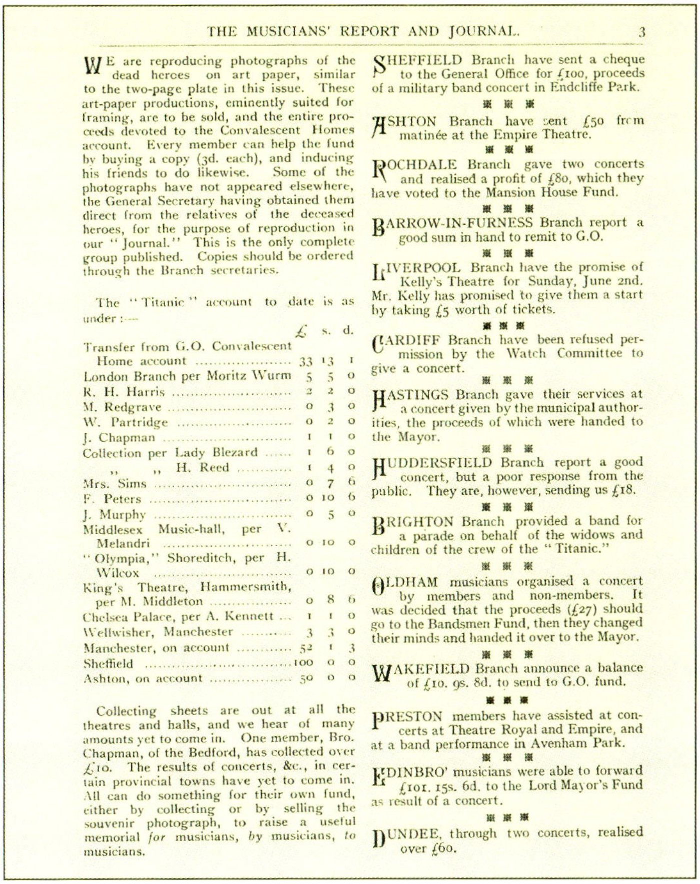
THE MUSICIANS' REPORT AND JOURNAL. 3

WE are reproducing photographs of the dead heroes on art paper, similar to the two-page plate in this issue. These art-paper productions, eminently suited for framing, are to be sold, and the entire proceeds devoted to the Convalescent Homes account. Every member can help the fund by buying a copy (3d. each), and inducing his friends to do likewise. Some of the photographs have not appeared elsewhere, the General Secretary having obtained them direct from the relatives of the deceased heroes, for the purpose of reproduction in our "Journal." This is the only complete group published. Copies should be ordered through the Branch secretaries.

The "Titanic" account to date is as under:—

	£	s.	d.
Transfer from G.O. Convalescent Home account	33	13	1
London Branch per Moritz Wurm	5	5	0
R. H. Harris	2	2	0
M. Redgrave	0	3	0
W. Partridge	0	2	0
J. Chapman	1	1	0
Collection per Lady Blezard	1	6	0
,, ,, H. Reed	1	4	0
Mrs. Sims	0	7	6
F. Peters	0	10	6
J. Murphy	0	5	0
Middlesex Music-hall, per V. Melandri	0	10	0
"Olympia," Shoreditch, per H. Wilcox	0	10	0
King's Theatre, Hammersmith, per M. Middleton	0	8	6
Chelsea Palace, per A. Kennett	1	1	0
Wellwisher, Manchester	3	3	0
Manchester, on account	52	1	3
Sheffield	100	0	0
Ashton, on account	50	0	0

Collecting sheets are out at all the theatres and halls, and we hear of many amounts yet to come in. One member, Bro. Chapman, of the Bedford, has collected over £10. The results of concerts, &c., in certain provincial towns have yet to come in. All can do something for their own fund, either by collecting or by selling the souvenir photograph, to raise a useful memorial *for* musicians, *by* musicians, *to* musicians.

SHEFFIELD Branch have sent a cheque to the General Office for £100, proceeds of a military band concert in Endcliffe Park.

ASHTON Branch have sent £50 from matinée at the Empire Theatre.

ROCHDALE Branch gave two concerts and realised a profit of £80, which they have voted to the Mansion House Fund.

BARROW-IN-FURNESS Branch report a good sum in hand to remit to G.O.

LIVERPOOL Branch have the promise of Kelly's Theatre for Sunday, June 2nd. Mr. Kelly has promised to give them a start by taking £5 worth of tickets.

CARDIFF Branch have been refused permission by the Watch Committee to give a concert.

HASTINGS Branch gave their services at a concert given by the municipal authorities, the proceeds of which were handed to the Mayor.

HUDDERSFIELD Branch report a good concert, but a poor response from the public. They are, however, sending us £18.

BRIGHTON Branch provided a band for a parade on behalf of the widows and children of the crew of the "Titanic."

OLDHAM musicians organised a concert by members and non-members. It was decided that the proceeds (£27) should go to the Bandsmen Fund, then they changed their minds and handed it over to the Mayor.

WAKEFIELD Branch announce a balance of £10. 9s. 8d. to send to G.O. fund.

PRESTON members have assisted at concerts at Theatre Royal and Empire, and at a band performance in Avenham Park.

EDINBRO' musicians were able to forward £101. 15s. 6d. to the Lord Mayor's Fund as result of a concert.

DUNDEE, through two concerts, realised over £60.

Page from the *Musicians' Journal*, June 1912, showing the donations received from various organisations and individuals.
Courtesy Musicians' Union Archive, Stirling University.

that Mr Sinclair, of the bank, refused to issue a cheque unless all the money was withdrawn and the account closed down. With Andrew writing letters saying he had proof that John wasn't the father, it made the whole saga very messy. It can only be assumed that the loss of his eldest son in such tragic circumstances had hit him much harder than anyone realised.

Andrew took the matter to court yet again on 27th January 1914, this time saying that he had definitive proof that John wasn't the father. He still maintained that the money from the *Titanic* fund in Liverpool was his personal claim. Sheriff Campion decided that he was not going to reopen the case.

The final instalment of this story was played out two weeks later, on Thursday 12th February, this time with Mary being represented by Mr Bannerman of Walker and Sharpe. At this hearing Mr Hendrie was being called as a witness therefore it was felt that he wouldn't be able to do the case justice if he was also acting as Mary's representative. When Mr Hendrie was questioned by Mr Edgar, he carefully went back over the whole case which tied in with everything Mary had said all along. The next witness was Andrew's previous solicitor Mr Henderson. He denied authorising Andrew to write any letters on his behalf. Mr Henderson then said it was because of these letters that he stopped representing Andrew. It was now the turn of Percy Corkhill, who had travelled up from Liverpool to attend. He brought with him a file that contained all of the correspondence between Andrew and the Relief Fund, and also had with him the minute book of committee meetings. The actual contents of the minute book were not in the end shown to the court as it was deemed unnecessary. There was, however, one moment of light relief when Mr Corkhill said to Sheriff Campion, regarding Andrew's numerous letters, I am sorry to trouble you. "As I am unacquainted with Scotch law I cannot quite follow the letters of Mr Hume". The courtroom burst into laughter! With Mr Corkhill having now read out some details from the minute book it was clear to all concerned that Andrew was, to say the least, complicating the issue. At this time Mr Edgar felt he had no alternative but to withdraw completely from the case.

It was decided that the hearing couldn't be adjourned, due to the logistics of Mr Corkhill returning to Dumfries from Liverpool. Andrew was given time to consult with Mr Edgar, who advised him to consent to the payment of the £67 2s. Once back in the courtroom, Sheriff Campion told Andrew that his actions, in trying to keep funds that were clearly meant for Mary, amounted to fraud. In the end it was decided that Andrew had to pay Mary the money from the fund, in addition to her keeping the money from the Boston fund, but Andrew faced no action against him. This brought an end to a case that was the talk of Dumfries from the very first hearing and was covered comprehensively in the *Dumfries and Galloway Standard* throughout. The 14th February 1914 edition carried the headline "*TITANIC* FUND CASE, DEFENDER'S AGENT WITHDRAWS. A SENSATIONAL ENDING", and the story itself covered several columns.

Whilst all this was being played out in the court, plans were beginning to be drawn up for a memorial to John Hume and Thomas Mullin. An Aberdeen granite obelisk, sixteen feet tall, to be situated a few yards from the bandstand in the Dock Park was agreed upon. It was estimated that the project would cost between £107 and £110. In total, £120 was collected from various sources, including £23 2s 5d from the boy scouts. On Saturday 31st May 1914 the memorial was unveiled in front of a large crowd; many had made a long journey especially for the occasion. Andrew, Alice and Catherine, along with members of the Mullin family, were present. It is not known if Mary attended.

Memorial and Bandstand in Dock Park, Dumfries.

Prior to the ceremony, the town band played *Nearer My God To Thee* while flags on the Midsteeple in the centre of the town and the town hall were flown at half mast. The unveiling was conducted by Provost Thompson of Dumfries and Provost Nicholson from Maxwelltown, both men wearing their robes and chains of office. Afterwards Reverend Strachan led the prayers, poignant as he had known John for most of his life. Now the Hume and Costin families had somewhere to go and pay their respects.

In memoriam postcard of the band members of the *Titanic*.

Probably the most fitting epitaph that could be paid to John and the musicians as a whole was a letter sent to the *Dumfries & Galloway Standard* on 24th April 1912, from a person signing themselves as just A. P. W. Dublin. It is apparent from the content that this was a letter from someone that had shared their childhood and friendship with John. The words are just as emotive and heartfelt today as they were when they first appeared in print, just days after the tragedy. Here is an extract: "There, standing ready to disembark on the very shores of eternity, the little band of hero musicians assembled for the last time. Their selection of *Nearer To God* was an appropriate one. Who shall say that the Almighty was not at that moment hovering over them ready to gather them unto himself? Johnny has gone and his violin silenced for ever; yet while memory keeps its seat that sad sweet solemn strain of the last hymn he helped play shall be wafted to us across the intervening ocean of time. Our eyes may become misty at the sound of the ghostly strain and we will grow sad to think such a young man has gone but our hearts will glow with pride when we remember the grand heroic order of his going".

Epilogue

The sequence of events that unfolded from the sinking of *Titanic* to the court hearings took its toll on the family. John's sister Catherine, in particular, found it very traumatic and it took her some considerable time to come to terms with the loss of both her mother to cancer and John in the sinking. The other members of the family gradually moved on with their lives. Nellie continued her career as a music teacher. Grace became a nurse and worked for a while at Huddersfield Hospital in Yorkshire and it is not known if she had any children. Catherine, although musically talented, worked for a while as a clerk in Dumfries. Later she entered service at a house in Bridge of Weir in Renfrewshire and it was while she was working there that she met and married train driver Thomas Terbit. The couple had five children, two daughters and three sons. The youngest son was named John Law Hume Terbit. Catherine died on 10th December 1947 at the age of 50 from lung disease. By that time she and Thomas had been living in Rutherglen (now part of Glasgow but at that time an ancient royal burgh and part of Lanarkshire.)

John's father, stepmother Alice and my grandfather moved from George Street, Dumfries in 1915 and settled in Great Portland Street, Westminster, London. Andrew set up as a violin maker and repairer as well as teaching music. They continued to live here until Andrew's death on 21st March 1934 from a brain haemorrhage, at which time he was a patient in Charing Cross Hospital in Agar Street, just off The Strand. Following Andrew's death, Alice moved back to Scotland, this time to Edinburgh, where her sister, Fanny, lived. Alice died from heart disease at home in Dundas Street, Edinburgh on 12th April 1939 aged 74 with her sister at her bedside.

In 1917 Walter Thompson, a Private with the British Expeditionary Force in Northern France, was on leave in Dumfries. Mary was working in the Arrol-Johnston car factory on the outskirts of the town. They met and fall in love, but it wasn't until the following year on 12th December that they married. The ceremony was conducted in the Costin family home in Buccleuch Street, Dumfries. The couple had two sons, Walter and Kennedy born in 1919 and 1921 respectively. Mary died from tuberculosis on 6th November 1922 at the age of 31. At the time the family were living in St. Andrew Street, Dumfries.

Arrol-Johnston factory, Dumfries.

After Mary's death Johnann went to live with her grandmother, Susan Costin at 35 Buccleuch Street. Johnann never had any further contact with her two half-brothers ever again. When Susan died on 10th July 1924 Johnann went to live with her uncle, Mary's younger brother Menzies and his wife. This was a very unhappy time for her and when she was in her teens she ran away to London, severing all ties with Dumfries for the rest of her life. She had a number of jobs; members of her family have suggested that this was in service which would have provided a job and a home. That she became very well-versed in social etiquette would support this. Around this time Johnann changed her name to Jacqueline but kept Law Hume as her middle names. In 1936 she married a journalist from the *London Evening News* and went on to have two children, a daughter born in 1938 and a son in 1942. Her husband died from a brain tumour in 1945 and she was left to bring up the two children on her own. Soon after the Second World War she got a job as a publicist for stars of the stage and screen, notably Anna Neagle and Herbert Wilcox. Jacqueline carried on with this kind of work until her late seventies; she had certainly inherited a spirit of adventure from her father! She died in 1995 at the age of 83.

By the time the court case regarding alimony for Johnann had come to an end my grandfather, Andrew, was nearing the end of his schooling. After living in London with Andrew and Alice for a few years he returned to Scotlandto pursue a career in music, the piano being his instrument of choice. As a professional musician he toured with his band as 'Andy Hume and his boys' until the outbreak of the Second World War. On a number of occasions he appeared in Harry Kemp's shows at the 'Cosy Corner' in the Clyde Coast resort of Dunoon. He married, but his first wife died in an accident.

On 8th August 1936, the day before what would have been John's 46th birthday, he married Margaret Skeet who worked as a shorthand typist. They had one daughter, my mother. Whilst serving in North Africa with the Royal Artillery during the war he was captured and spent time as a prisoner of war in Italy. Some years after the end of the war my grandfather emigrated to Australia where he spent the rest of his life.

Millvina Dean

Elizabeth Gladys (Millvina) Dean was born on 2nd February 1912 and she went on to become the youngest and last surviving passenger on RMS *Titanic*. At the time of sailing Millvina was accompanied by her mother Georgette Eva, father Bertram Frank and brother Bertram Vere aged two. Millvina's parents wished to emigrate from England to America and start a new life. Bertram Frank's relatives lived in Wichita, Kansas and it was decided that they would settle nearby and maybe open a tobacconist shop.

It was a sad fate for the Dean family as they were not originally booked onto the *Titanic*, but they were booked onto the *Philadelphia*. However, following a coal strike they were transferred to *Titanic* and boarded as third class passengers. On that fateful night in April 1912 Millvina's mother was in the cabin with her young sleeping children whilst her father, Bertram Frank, was up on deck. On feeling the impact of the iceberg Bertram Frank rushed to his family's cabin and told his wife Georgette, "quickly dress the children in warm clothes, we need to go to the lifeboat deck". Georgette immediately did as her husband requested. Millvina, together with her mother and brother, were eventually placed into a lifeboat and they were among the first passengers to leave the sinking liner. Millvina's father did not go with his family into the lifeboat and he eventually perished. Bertram Frank's body was never identified, adding to the grief of the Dean family.

Georgette and her two young children were eventually rescued from their lifeboat by the *Carpathia* and taken to New York City. The family eventually returned to England on *Adriatic*. Millvina was just two months old at this time and she was so adorable that she became the 'pet of the liner'. There were so many keen women queuing to hold the beautiful tiny baby that an officer had to order, "first and second class passengers may hold the infant for no more than two minutes"! Millvina's grieving mother wanted to continue the wishes of her husband and still emigrate to Kansas, but with two young children to raise on her own, she couldn't cope financially. Millvina and her brother went on to be raised mainly on pension funds.

As a young woman Millvina worked for the British government during the Second World War, then later for an engineering firm. She also worked as a secretary, a cartographer and as an assistant to a tobacconist. Millvina never married and dedicated herself to caring for her ailing mother, who died at the age of 96 on 16th September 1975. Her brother Bertram Vere died in 1992 at the age of 82.

Millvina became the last surviving passenger of the *Titanic* following the death of Barbara West Dainton on 16th October 2007, aged 96. Barbara was just ten months old as a *Titanic* passenger.

Millvina passed away peacefully in her sleep on 31st May 2009 – 98 years to the day from the launch of the *Titanic*. Although Millvina knew, from the age of eight, that she had been a *Titanic* passenger, she didn't really think too much about it until she came into the spotlight in 1985. This is when Doctor Robert Ballard discovered the location of the *Titanic* wreck. It was then that the media went 'full steam ahead' and wanted to find all survivors. Following this rise to fame Millvina, now in her seventies, went on to attend *Titanic* conventions, appeared on televison and radio and travelled all over the world, along with her trusted friend and companion Bruno.

When I wrote to Millvina in early 2008, I was absolutely delighted to receive an invitation to meet her and on 13th July 2008 I arrived at her nursing home in Southampton. I was quite anxious, but also excited to be meeting a woman, now 96, who carried with her such history.

When I entered her room, the first thing that struck me was how tiny and frail she looked. I didn't know quite what to expect, but once we started talking it wasn't long before I was swept into the life of this remarkable woman. She was kindness itself, extremely interesting, intelligent and with a great sense of humour. I soon forgot that I was speaking to a woman of such mature years. She told me in great detail of her life and of course, the sadness at losing her father so tragically. She went on to show me photographs of her family and quite rightly, she was very proud of her handsome father.

I was fascinated by the many soft teddy bears and humorous dancing toys that dominated her room; she told me that they were gifts from the many people that she had met over the years. She even remembered the name of each person whom the gift was from! What also impressed me was how hard she was still working. On a chair there was a huge pile of letters and books for her to sign; she never let anyone down and worked through them with a great sense of duty to those who had taken the trouble to write to her.

The meeting was however tinged with sadness as Millvina explained how she was struggling financially to meet the costs of her nursing home bills. She felt that she needed to raise funds and therefore it had been decided that she would sell a wicker suitcase of donated clothing (given to her mother following the *Titanic* sinking) plus other items. Her plight attracted a lot of media attention and she was on the news and in the national newspapers for quite a while. This was second nature to Millvina as she had been in the spotlight many times before and was a natural! This much-needed media attention highlighted her situation and at auction in late 2008, although she only expected to raise a few thousand pounds, fortunately and to my great relief, she managed to raise around £31,000. I was so very pleased for her when I heard the good news. When asked how she felt about having to sell personal belongings she, in her very commonsense and level-headed way said, "you have to do what you have to do".

I was very moved to be in the company of someone who was actually in the same place, at the same time, as my great uncle, John Hume. It made me feel closer to him. Millvina was in turn very enthusiastic to meet me as she had great respect for the band on the *Titanic*. She was also thrilled to be contributing a foreword for this book.

I will always treasure the memory and privilege of spending time with dear Millvina. A memorial service was held for Millvina on 24th October 2009 at St. Mary's Church Copythorne, taken by Reverend Neville Jacob who also had officiated at Millvina's funeral. At 1pm her ashes were scattered onto the water of berth 43/44 in Southampton Docks, from where she had set sail on *Titanic* 97 years before.

Liner dock, Southampton. On the left is a Red Star liner, beyond which is the *Olympic*. On the right are Cunard's *Mauritania*, with *Aquitania* beyond.

REPERTOIRE.

Overtures.

1	Il Barbiere di Siviglia	*Rossini*
2	Zampa	*Herold*
3	Semiramide	*Rossini*
4	La Gazza ladra	"
5	Muta di Portici	*Auber*
6	Italiana in Algeri	*Rossini*
7	Tancredi	"
8	Guglielmo Tell	"
9	Morning, Noon and Night in Vienna	*Suppè*
10	Pique Dame	"
11	Poet and Peasant	"
12	Raymond	*A. Thomas*
13	Martha	*Flotow*
14	Agnes	*F. Paer*
15	The Bohemian Girl ...	*Balfe*

Operatic Selections, etc.

16	The Quaker Girl	*Monckton*
17	The Girl in the Train	*Leo. Fall*
18	Samson and Delilah	*St. Saëns*
19	Madame Sherry ..	*K. Hoschna*
20	Cadix	*Valverde*
21	Aïda	*Verdi*
22	Thaïs	*Massenet*
23	The Chocolate Soldier	*O. Strauss*
24	Cavalleria Rusticana ...	*Mascagni*
25	Mignon	*Thomas*
26	Un Ballo in Maschera	*Verdi*
27	Pagliacci	*Leoncavallo*
28	Orphee Aux Enfers	*Offenbach*
29	Madam Butterfly	*Puccini*
30	The Dollar Princess ..	*Leo Fall*
31	A Waltz Dream	*O. Straus*
32	Miss Hook of Holland	*Rubens*
33	The Merry Widow	*Lehar*
34	Our Miss Gibbs	*Monckton*
35	The Arcadians	"
36	The Belle of Brittany	*Talbot*
37	Havana	*Stuart*

2

38 Dear Little Denmark ... ... *Rubens*
39 The Fair Co-ed .. ... *Luder*
40 The Grand Mogul .. ... "
41 The Gay Musician ... *Julian Edward*
42 A Trip to Japan ... ... *Klein*
43 His Honour the Mayor .. *Julian Edward*
44 The Red Mill .. ... *V Herbert*
45 The Prima Donna ... ... "
46 The Three Twins ... ... *Karl Hoschna*
47 The Prince of Pilsen .. .. *Luder*
48 It Happened in Nordland .. *V. Herbert*
49 Neptune's Daughter .. "
50 Faust .. ... *Gounod*
51 Carmen .. .. *Bizet*
52 Il Trovatore ... . *Verdi*
53 Rigoletto .. .. "
54 La Traviata .. .. .. "
55 Puritani ... . *Bellini*
56 La Sonnambula ... ... "
57 Lucia di Lammermoor .. ... *Donizetti*
58 La Favorita ... ... "
59 Tosca ... ... *Puccini*
60 La Bohéme .. .. "
61 The Mikado .. .. .. *Sullivan*
62 Pirates of Penzance ... .. "
63 Iolanthe .. .. "
64 A Princess of Kensington . *E. German*
65 Merrie England .. .. "
66 Tom Jones ... ... "
67 Manon Lescaut ... .. *Puccini*
68 Les Contes D'Hoffman ... .. *Offenbach*
69 Mefistofele ... ... *Boito*
70 Tannhauser ... ... *Wagner*
71 Lohengrin .. .. "
72 The Girls of Gottenburg ... *Caryll & Monckton*
73 Haddon Hall ... ... *Sullivan*
74 The Gondoliers .. ... "
75 Recollections of Gounod .. .. *Godfrey*
76 Sullivan's Melodies .. ... "
77 The Maid and the Mummy *A. Aarons*
78 Love's Lottery ... *Julian Edwards*
79 M'lle Modisté .. .. .. "
80 Miss Dolly Dollars .. .. "
81 Wonderland .. .. "

3

82 The Princess Beggar ... *A. G. Robyn*
83 The Geisha ... . *Jones*
84 San Toy .. .. "

Suites, Fantasias, etc.

85 Peer Gynt Suite .. .. *Greig*
86 Three Dances: "Henry VIII" .. *E. German*
87 Three Dances: "Nell Gwyn" .. "
88 Three Dances: "Tom Jones" ... "
89 The Rose .. .. *Myddleton*
90 The Thistle .. .. "
91 The Shamrock .. ... "
92 American National Airs .. *Tobani*
93 Plantation Songs ... . *Clutsam*
94 Canadian Songs ... . *Retford*
95 Tosti's Popular Songs .. ... *Godfrey*
96 Popular Songs .. .. .. *S. Adams*
97 Reminiscences of the Savoy ... *M. Moore*
98 Reminiscences of Wales .. *Godfrey*
99 Reminiscences of All Nations "
100 National Anthems, Hymns, etc., of all Nations.

Waltzes.

101 Love and Life in Holland ... *Joyce*
102 Partners Galore ... . *G. V*
103 The Druid's Prayer .. *Davson*
104 Vision of Salome ... . *Joyce*
105 Remembrance ... . "
106 Beautiful Spring . .. ... *Lincke*
107 Wedding Dance .. .. "
108 Comedie d'Amour ... ... *G. Colin*
109 Valse Septembre .. ... *F. Godwin*
110 Mondaine ... . *Bosc*
111 Réve d'Artiste .. .. "
112 Swing Song .. .. *Hollaender*
113 Sphinx .. .. *Popy*
114 Songe d'Automne .. .. *Joyce*
115 La Lettre de Manon .. ... *Giliet*
116 Cecilia ... ... *Pether*
117 Apach's Dance .. .. *Offenbach*
118 Verschmähte Liebe ... ... *P. Lincke*
119 Lysistrata ... ... "
120 Luna ... ... "

4

121 L'Heure Suprême .. ... *A. Lotter*
122 Rouge et Noir ... ... "
123 Sans-Souci ... . *Von Blon*
124 Sizilietta ... . "
125 Gold and Silver ... ... *Lehar*
126 Amorettentänze .. .. *Gung'l*
127 Die Hydropaten ... . "
128 Venus Reigen ... .. "
129 Jungherren Tänze .. "
130 Mein Schönster Tag in Berlin .. "
131 Soldaten-Lieder ... "
132 Früthlingslieder ... "
133 Dreams on the Ocean .. "
134 Zephyr-Lüfte ... ... "
135 Casino Tänze ... ... "
136 Elfen Reigen ... ... "
137 Immortellen ... ... "
138 An der Schönen Blauen Donau *Strauss*
139 Morgenblätter ... . "
140 Hofballtänze ... ... "
141 Wiener Blut ... ... "
142 Promotionen .. .. "
143 Tausend und eine Nacht "
144 Freuet euch des Lebens... .. "
145 Geschichten Aus Dem Wiener Wald "
146 Künstler Leben ... ... "
147 Leitartikel ... ... "
148 Doctrinen .. .. "
149 Wein Weib und Gesang.. ... "
150 Tresor D'Amour ... ... *Waldteufel*
151 The Grenadiers .. .. "
152 Solitude .. .. "
153 Bien Aimés .. "
154 Flots de Joie ... "
155 Reine des Coeurs... ... "
156 Abandon ... ... *Waldtenfel*
157 Hommage aux Dames ... .. "
158 Entre Nous ... ... "
159 Estudiantina ... ... "
160 La Source ... ... "
161 La Barcarole ... ... "
162 The White Star Line Waltz, *J. C. H. Beaumont*
163 A Waltz Dream ... *O. Straus*
164 The Merry Widow .. *Lehar*

5

Sacred Music.

165 Selections from Elijah . ... *Mendelssohn*
166 " The Cross of Calvary. *Gounod*
167 " Stabat Mater .. *Rossini*
168 " The Messiah ... *Handel*
169 Song—For all Eternity ... *Mascheroni*
170 Ave Maria ... "
171 War March of the Priests .. *Mendelssohn*
172 March of the Israelites .. .. *Costa*

Entr'actes, Intermezzos, etc.

173 Ave Maria ... ... *Gounod*
174 Angel's Serenade.. .. .. *Braga*
175 Anvil Chorus from Il-Trovatore *Verdi*
176 Apple Blossoms ... . *Roberts*
177 Amaryllis ... . *Ghys*
178 Cavalieria Rusticana, Intermezzo *Mascagni*
179 Entre Act Gavotte from Mignon *Thomas*
180 Fifth Hungarian Dance .. ... *Brahms*
181 First Heart Throbs .. *Eilenberg*
182 Flower Song ... . *Lange*
183 La Morsaria ... .. *Morse*
184 La Paloma... .. .. *Yradier*
185 Loin Du Bal ... ... *Gillett*
186 Love's Dream after the Ball .. *Czibulka*
187 Marguerite Waltzes from Faust *Gounod*
188 Minuet .. .. *Paderewski*
189 Pizzacato Polka ... .. *Strauss*
190 Prize Song from Die Meistersinger *Wagner*
191 Serenade .. .. *Schubert*
192 Sextette from Lucia .. ... *Donizetti*
193 Simple Aveu .. .. *Thome*
194 Spring Song ... ... *Mendelssohn*
195 Turkish Patrol ... .. *Michaelis*
196 Traumerei .. .. *Schumann*
197 Zallah ... ... *Loraine*
198 Anitra's Dance .. ... *Grieg*
199 Amaranthus ... ... *Gilder*
200 Barcarolle, Tales of Hoffmann... *Offenbach*
201 Berceuse from Jocelyn ... *Godard*
202 Calm as the Night ... *Bohm*
203 Confidence... ... ... *Mendelssohn*

6

204 Entre Acte .. .. *Gillet*
205 O Star of Eve, from Tannhauser *Wagner*
206 Guardmount Patrol .. *Eilenberg*
207 Flatterer, The ... .. *Chaminade*
208 Funeral March of a Marionette *Gounod*
209 Hungarian Dance No. 2 .. *Brahms*
210 Intermezzo Russe .. .. *Franke*
211 Kaiser Frederic March .. .. *Friedeman*
212 Largo .. *Handel*
213 Nocturne Op. 9, No. 2 *Chopin*
214 Panquita, Danza Mexicana *Robyn*
215 Pizzicati from Sylvia ... *Delibes*
216 Quartette from Rigoletto .. *Verdi*
217 Rakoczy, Hungarian March ... *Liszt*
218 Scarf Dance .. ... *Chaminade*
219 Serenade .. .. *Pierne*
220 Song Without Words .. .. *Tschaikowsky*
221 Spanish Dance No. 1 .. .. *Moszkowski*
222 Stephanie Gavotte *Czibulka*
223 Czardas (No. 1) .. *Michiels*
224 " (No. 2) .. "
225 " (No. 3) "
226 " (No. 4) ... "
227 " (No. 5) .. .. "
228 " (No. 6) "
229 Pantins Vivants ... .. *Leoncavallo*
230 Husheen .. .. *Needham*
231 Violets .. *Ellen Wright*
232 L'Extase ... .. *Thomé*
233 Andante Religioso "
234 The Rosary .. .. *Nevin*
235 Humoreske .. *Dvorák*
236 Dreams .. ... *Wagner*
237 Agnus Dei ... . *Bizet*
238 I Love Thee .. *Grieg*
239 None but the weary heart *Tschaikovski*
240 La Gitanette .. *Valverde*
241 La Tzigane .. .. .. *Ganne*
242 La Czarine .. .. .. "
243 Danse du Paraquay ... *Valverde*
244 Amina .. .. *Lincke*
245 Awakening of Love .. *Lotter*
246 Miss Antique ... .. *Trinkaus*
247 Glow Worm .. ... *Lincke*

7

248 Hearts and Flowers .. *Tobani*
249 Forget-me-not ... .. *Macbeth*
250 Anona ... .. *V Grey*
251 Serenade d'Amour .. .. *Von Blon*
252 The Gondolier .. .. *Powell*
253 Andante Cantabile ... *Tschaikovski*
254 Narcissus .. .. *Nevin*
255 Liebestraum .. *Von Blon*
256 La Berceuse .. *Gounod*
257 Melody in F .. *Rubinstein*
258 Salut d'Amour .. ... *Elgar*
259 Blumengeflüster .. *Von Blon*
260 Menuet .. .. *Boccherini*
261 Cavatina .. .. *Raff*
262 Poppies .. .. .. *N. Moret*
263 Eventide .. ... *W H. Myddleton*
264 Gavotte ... "Herz an Herz" ... *Latann*
265 Traum de Sennerin .. .. *Labitzky*
266 On the Banks of Allan Water ... *E. Jones*
267 Malena .. .. *M. Ellis*
268 The Teddy Bear's Picnic *J. W. Bratton*
269 Alfresco .. ... *Victor Herbert*
270 Captain Cupid .. *J. W Bratton*
271 In a Pagoda ... ... "
272 Araby .. .. *Al. Johns*
273 Salome ... ... *Lorrainè*
274 In a Lotus Field .. .. *W. Bratton*
275 The Whistler and his Dog .. *Pryor*
276 Spangles .. .. *J. W. Bratton*
277 Roses and Memories .. *Snyder*

Marches, Cake Walks, etc.

278 Kwang Hsu .. *Lincke*
279 Siamese Patrol ... . "
280 The Ladybird's Review ... *Moret*
281 The Coons' Patrol .. *Lotter*
282 The Cadet .. ... *Haines*
283 Buy Jingo .. ... *Thurban*
284 Paris à New York .. *Detrain*
285 Strauss .. .. *Mezzocapo*
286 A Bunch of Roses .. *Chapi*
287 Cherries .. .. *Cremieux*
288 The Baby Parade .. *Pryor*

8

289 Marche de Madrid .. ... *Valverde*
290 Le Prophêté ... ... *Meyerbeer*
291 Tannhauser .. *Wagner*
292 Pomp and Circumstance, No. 1 *Elgar*
293 " " No. 2 "
294 " " No. 4 "
295 Marche Algérienne ... *Bosc*
296 Le Pére La Victorie ... ... *Ganne*
297 The Peace Maker .. *Lotter*
298 The Light Horse *Von Blon*
299 With the British Colours ... *F. Von Blon*
300 Rakoczy .. .. *S. V Balfour*
301 Le Regiment Favori .. *D. Erti*
302 Castaldo ... .. *R. Novacék*
303 Under the Double Eagle *F. Wagner*
304 The Last Stand .. *W. H. Myddleton*
305 Through Night to Light ... *E. Lankien*
306 Sounds of Peace ... .. *Von Blon*
307 Viscount Nelson ... ... *W Zehle*
308 Manuella .. ... *Lotter*
309 Entry of the Gladiators ... .. *Fucêk*
310 La Petite Tonkinoise .. *Scotto and Christine*
311 Hobomoko .. ... *Reeves*
312 Yankee Grit ... . *Holzmann*
313 Berliner Lüft ... .. *Lincke*
314 Hail, Spirit of Liberty! ... *Sousa*
315 Hands Across the Sea .. "
316 The Bride Elect ... "
317 The Invincible Eagle .. "
318 The Charlatan .. .. "
319 Stars and Stripes for Ever .. "
320 El Capitan ... ... "
321 Manhattan Beach ... .. "
322 Gaily through the World ... *Macbeth*
323 The Drum Major ... *James*
324 Four-in-hand ... *Braham*
325 Frivolity .. .. *Macquinn*
326 Jolly Clowns .. ... *Whitney*
327 Bill Simmons *Spink*
328 Silverheels .. .. *Moret*
329 Rainbow ... ... *Wenrich*
330 Old Daddy Pegleg ... .. *Whitney*
331 Uncle Dudley ... .. *Kellogg*
332 Prosit .. .. *Fessler*

9

333 Sakes Alive .. .. *S. Howard*
334 Indian Patrol .. ... *H. Witney*
335 My Ivy Vine .. .. "
336 Facing the Music *Soucoup*
337 Lilliputia .. .. *Rogers*
338 Mocking Bird Rube .. *Wm. Syers*
339 By Right of Sword .. .. *Theo. Bendix*
340 Lumb'rin' Luke ... *Silberberry*
341 Nigger Alley .. .. *Andrews*
342 H. I. M. .. .. .. *Myddleton*
343 Yip-i-addy-i-ay .. *Higgs*
344 Polka, Jeu d'Esprit ... *Waldteufel*
345 " L'Esprit Francaise "
346 " Bonne Bouche .. "
347 " En Garde .. ... "
348 " Bagatelle .. "
349 " Camarade .. "
350 " Par-ci-par-la .. .. "
351 " Minuet .. .. "
352 Hello Girls .. *J H. Beaumont*

ACKNOWLEDGEMENTS

Roger Findlay, Norfolk
Research, photography and constant support

Hilda Hume, Suffolk
Family insight and photographs

Jean & Roy Flowerdew
Photographs and ephemera for the White Star Line and musicians.

Richard Stenlake, Scotland
Illustrations, friendly support and valued help throughout.

Thomas Stanley, England.
Photograph of the Cable Ship Mackay Bennett.

Michael and Nicola Greaves, France
French translation

Graham Roberts Neil Moffat - Cath Aitken - Erica Johnson - Kathy Gibb:
Ewart Library, Dumfries and Galloway, Scotland
Excellent research team & support throughout

Hazel Clement, Met office
Detailed Dumfries weather statistics

Gary Shutlack, Chief Archivist (NSARM) Canada
Archive research and document tracing

St. Michael's Street school; Dumfries and Galloway, Scotland
Accommodating with photography assistance

Karl Magee
Musician's union extracts,
University archivist, University of Stirling, Scotland

Victoria Brown
National Archive of Scotland, Edinburgh

David Inkster
General registrar of Scotland, Edinburgh